Lumberjack Jesus

How to Develop Faith Despite Pitfalls, Roadblocks,
Stupidity and Prejudice

Bruce Kirkpatrick

WD
PUBLISHING

Green Bay, WI 54311

Editor: Brittiany Koren
Cover Art Design and Layout: Ed Vincent of ENC Graphic Services
Cover image: © PiXXart/Shutterstock
Category: Christian Men's Memoir/Non-Fiction
Description: How to develop faith despite pitfalls, roadblocks, stupidity, and prejudice. Insightful and uplifting, *Lumberjack Jesus* is a memoir by Bruce Kirkpatrick that reminds us all that we need and deserve unconditional love.

Hardcover ISBN: 978-0-9962521-4-0
Paperback ISBN: 978-0-9962521-5-7
Ebook ISBN: 978-0-9962521-6-4

LOC: Catalog info applied for.

First Edition published by Written Dreams Publishing in July 2016.

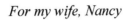

For my wife, Nancy

Introduction

Belief in God did not come easy for me. For two-thirds of my life, I resisted him, fought against him, and ignored him.

And yet, he always seemed to be around.

These are stories of how I developed a faith in God. Some are reflections on times in my life before God entered it, and seeing now how He was actually present even though I wasn't aware of it. Some stories I've never told a soul before I wrote them down here for the first time. Those contain my life's secrets, some dark, some downright devilish, some bleak, and some beckoning for help from a God I hadn't yet met. I was crying out in the dark to something or *someone* for help. God was the only one that answered.

Some of these stories illustrate how I came to know God and to trust Him; He showed me the errors of my youth. My self-indulgent, narcissistic actions and thoughts gradually fell away, discarded trash piles of younger days. He changed me for the better. He taught me to love and how to accept others. He taught me to cry over the things that broke his heart. And, just as important, He taught me how to forgive myself and fall back in love with the man He originally created, born to this Earth in 1951. No small feat.

For those of you who have not discovered God or think that He doesn't exist, this book is for you. I believe it will give you hope. Hope in a world that seems at times insane and completely without rhyme or reason, or where anyone is in charge. At least anyone in charge who knows what he's doing. Hope in a generous, benevolent God who is open and available to you, and still in control. If He can love and accept an uncaring, self-centered, lustful dope like me, He can do the same for you. Nobody is beyond His reach or His hand.

This book may also convince you that as a Christian, I can be as stupid, calloused, and prejudiced as anybody else. That will hopefully dispel the rumors out there that we Christians somehow think we are holier than you. We are not; I am *especially* not.

This book is not meant to be preachy. I don't point out how you should run your life. I simply point out the pitfalls I encountered in mine, and the lessons I learned (mostly the hard way) from those encounters. I reached deep down to discover why it is I believe in God and how He works in my everyday life, not just my Sunday go-to-meeting life. How I find Him in a drive along a congested freeway or atop a mountain in remote Wyoming. How He comes to life—real, present, almost human-like—in the slums of Haiti, by a firing squad in Utah, or near a rock concert named Woodstock. How He influenced me through my mother and my father (neither of whom knew Him intimately) or with Bobby Knight, the famed screeching general of a basketball coach.

If you don't know God, some of these stories may show you that He does indeed exist. I'll illustrate how I believe He saved me from such horrors as a car spinning down a freeway at 70 miles per hour backwards; from destroying my marriage by answering an email from an old girlfriend; or the shame and guilt from burying my sexual abuse for twenty-five years.

If you are a Christian, this book is for you, too. These stories will show you how I struggle with my faith, in the hope that by seeing my struggles, your struggles will become real, honest, human—and how Jesus can help you through the rough times. These stories may open new ways to think about God, react to Him, play with Him, be with Him, know Him, and dare I say, obey Him.

You may not agree with my theology or my spiritual habits, and that's okay. After all, I recently mothballed my prayer list and haven't attended church much in the last five years. But it is my hope, that God, and especially Jesus, may come alive to you in these pages as He did for me—in stories about Vietnam heroes, cowboy movies, wrestling matches and chemistry sets.

To me, God comes alive in everyday life. Not just in the Bible or in church. He is not simply a legalistic, ethereal character in the Bible. To me, Jesus looks like a lumberjack in a red plaid shirt, jeans and with a short-cropped beard. When I needed Him most—when I was consumed by anger, shame and guilt, and quite literally dying on the inside—Jesus visited me every day for three months and sat alongside me at my dining room table. There, I discovered how He loves me and cares for me. Even when I push Him away. So far away and with such belligerence and bellowing that you would be convinced that I neither deserved nor desired that love.

But you would be wrong. I do. You do, too. We all do.

Scripture:

"Christ Jesus came into the world to save sinners—of whom I am the worst. But for that very reason I was shown mercy so that in me, the worst of sinners, Christ Jesus might display his unlimited patience as an example for those who would believe on him and receive eternal life. Now to the King eternal, immortal, invisible, the only God, be honor and glory for ever and ever. Amen."

—1 Timothy, 1:15-17

Prayer:

Lord, may the words of my mouth and the meditations of my heart be pleasing to you. Work through me now. Holy Spirit come alive in me and may your passion, your voice and your love shine on me and through me. Thank you, sweet Jesus. Amen.

Lumberjack Jesus

My search for God has been a heart journey, an emotional quest. I'm sure my soul was involved, that someplace deep down inside of me I wanted and needed a connection with Him. I was never interested in discovering a historical God or even investigating other incarnations of God, like the ones proposed by the Mormon or Islamic religions. Religion itself has very little appeal to me. My quest has been to understand the God written about in the Bible, and my heart has always led in that journey.

My parents divorced when I was two years old, and I was predominately raised by women, my mother and grandmother. At times, it was difficult to develop into a man. There weren't many good, strong male role models around me. In the 1950s, men had returned victorious from the war, my dad included, and they were ready to sow their oats. The traditional family was still intact in America, but acting on the little seams of discontent that were always there began to tear at its fabric. Affairs happened, like they always had, but in my family, divorce followed, which was *not* always the case. It certainly wasn't accepted—not like it is today—but we weren't too far away from the free love generation of the 60s when many of society's traditions were tossed to the wind.

As a young boy, I was sexually molested by a family friend. I don't write that as casually as it may read. I never told a soul for twenty-five years and it only surfaced as I was writing my autobiography for a career counselor. I had stuffed the incident and emotions deep inside.

As I matured, the shame and guilt I felt over it often exploded out of me in anger. I didn't realize these emotional toxins I'd squashed were escaping with such force and suddenness.

I later realized I felt responsible for letting the abuse happen. I hated myself for not being man enough to stop it. Heavy burdens to bear as a young boy growing into a man. So I shouldered them alone; I buried them.

My church experience growing up did nothing to alleviate that guilt or shame. I attended Sunday school and church every other weekend, whenever we stayed with my father. As a young boy in grade school, I enjoyed Sunday school because I was with friends and it was fun.

When I graduated to the church service, I was bored out of my skull. The Presbyterian Church we attended was all adorned with flowing robes, ornate high ceilings, a choir that only sang dirges (they called them hymns) and to top it off, I was told to wear a shirt and tie. Every service. Ugh!

As far as I can remember, I never once heard the saving grace of Jesus Christ talked about in that church. Maybe I wasn't listening.

When I left for college at eighteen, I left the church. I only returned for special occasions—weddings and funerals—and never for a moment did I miss it. I stayed away for almost twenty years.

As I hit my mid-thirties, living the life of a self-proclaimed freewheeling bachelor, I began to feel loneliness creep into my life. For a long time, I relished the fact that I had left home, moved about as far away as I could from my family, and made my own way in life. What I didn't realize at the time was that I was searching for something to make me feel whole again.

I attended Werner Erhard's est training, Dale Carnegie courses, got into outside sales to prove my worth, and took just about every self-help seminar I could. I listened to every cassette tape series I could get my hands on. I felt better about myself, but I was still incomplete.

Then I met my future wife Nancy and decided I wanted to spend the rest of my life with her. Starting a relationship with that wonderful woman prepared me to start one with God.

We had our first child when I was thirty-five, our second at thirty-eight. As we looked at preschools, she picked the one closest to our home, with the nicest staff and the cleanest facility. It just happened to be a Christian school. God was reaching out to me again, but I still didn't hear Him.

One night at the dinner table, my youngest, about three years old at the time, asked where Jesus lived. Intellectually I scanned my limited Biblical knowledge, and answered, "In Heaven, with God." Pretty good, huh?

My oldest, who was six years old, politely corrected me and proclaimed, "No, Daddy. He lives in your heart."

My wife and I exchanged glances, and I said to her we had better check out what they were teaching our children at that school.

As Christ pursued us through our kids and a very upbeat, practical, heartfelt church and its congregation, we followed. My wife and I accepted Christ as our personal savior on the same Sunday in April of 1993. It felt right and good in our hearts.

But mine is a stubborn heart.

Even as God captured it, I resisted. Not in the typical ways of ignoring, rebelling or abstaining from Him. No, I continued to learn about God, read my Bible daily, and devoured Christian literature. I attended church classes and joined a small home group to get to know the people of God and understand Him better. I was in a small men's group with one of the pastors of the church. I volunteered everywhere in the church I could so I could see the longing in people's eyes searching for God, and the splendor in their lives when they found Him.

But I rarely cried out to God. I was still an angry man. I wanted to know God on a personal level, but I still felt the shame and guilt of what had happened thirty years earlier. It was a barrier between the two of us, Him and I. I wondered if I *was* this new being, this new creature, born again new and fresh, then why was I still so angry? Why hadn't my relationship with God and Jesus and all the loving people in my church cured my anger? I didn't understand it.

After having buried the abuse deep within me for so long, it had finally surfaced. That's what hit me hard.

I was writing an autobiography for the career counselor I was working with who wanted to know more about my past. When she saw the reference—hidden as a one-line description of my youth—she immediately recommended I dig deeper.

I wasn't thrilled by the idea at first. Poking in my past wasn't something I wanted to do, but I eventually found a terrific therapist who helped me understand and express what I was feeling. I told my wife and a few family members about the truth of what had happened all those years ago, how I had felt so vulnerable, and then I began to heal.

I learned that the more I spoke about "the incident" as I called it, the more I understood and accepted it.

As I was preparing a speech—that was to include small references of the abuse—to a church group one morning, reading Joel Osteen's book of *Your Best Year Now* daily devotionals, I encountered a reading about forgiveness. It *changed* my relationship with God.

The reading said that you don't forgive those people who have done you wrong, especially those terrible things done to you, for their sake. You forgive them for *your sake*. I hadn't realized I had been punishing myself for years with that guilt and shame. So I forgave myself that morning—and continued to do so many mornings to follow.

Gradually over time, I grew closer to God. I felt this great weight lifted off my shoulders and could literally feel my heart begin to soften. My anger subsided, but it never left. Not really. Something was still missing.

By this time in my life, I was ten years into my walk with Jesus. I was still empty at times and continued to experience explosions of anger erupting out of me. I had some serious anger management issues.

Then God worked in me through a book called *The Shack*. In this book, God, Jesus and the Holy Spirit are depicted not as ethereal non-beings, but are given the characteristics, mannerisms, clothes and appearances of real life people. Okay, so the Holy Spirit is fairy-like but still visible in shape and structure. Somehow, seeing Jesus as a man with a short-cropped beard and flannel shirt, looking very much like a lumberjack, hit the mark with me. I could *relate* because it made Him real; He seemed like an older brother.

So lumberjack Jesus and I began a conversation.

Not once in my ten years as a Christian had I ever heard God talk to me directly, in words I could hear (or at least distinguish), until those conversations. Early each morning for three months, the two of us spent time together at my dining room table, in serious give and take about anger, forgiveness, grace, the cross and love.

Lumberjack Jesus told me that my guilt and shame were keeping me from being the person He had originally created. He never used the word "sin", but I've come to realize that sin is simply that what keeps me from my relationship with Him, so now I label those feelings that way. Jesus never used that word. And He never required that I ask for forgiveness; I didn't need to come to Him and beg for mercy. He simply said that if I would relinquish the guilt and shame to Him, He would nail them to the cross. That was his job; that was why He came to Earth. Then, I could get back to being the man that He created.

It was a very visual depiction of the cross, a symbol of His sacrifice, but also a place where I could surrender my guilt and shame. I sometimes try to imagine how sturdy that cross is to be able to handle not only my sins, but also the sins of the world.

Gradually, over time, I asked Him to take away my guilt and shame. He smiled at me and reached for His hammer and nails.

SCRIPTURE:

"After Jesus said this, he looked toward heaven and prayed, 'Father, the time has come. Glorify your Son, that your Son may glorify you. For you granted him authority over all people that he might give eternal life to all those you have given him. Now this is eternal life: that they may know you, the only true God, and Jesus Christ, whom you have sent. I have brought you glory on earth by completing the work you gave me to do. And now, Father, glorify me in your presence and with the glory I had with you before the world began.' "

—John 17:1-5

PRAYER:

Dear heavenly Father, dear Lumberjack Jesus, I fall down on my knees at the cross. Thank you for your sacrifice for me. Yes, you sacrificed for the world, but thank you that I was included. Help me to remember you as an older brother or friend. Help me to visualize you next to me, ready to listen and understand me, ready to restore me. Make it easy for me to come to you to hand over my burdens, without having to beg or plead for forgiveness. Thank you for having an endless supply of nails and a cross ready to bear the weight of an unbelievable burden. Thank you, sweet Jesus. Amen.

The Chemistry Set

I don't remember my mother and father ever living together in the same house. I suppose that's not unusual, considering they divorced when I was two years old. My mom rented an apartment for a few years and when I was six, she bought, with the help of her parents, a home only a block from the apartment. It was within walking distance of my first school, a four-room schoolhouse housing grades one through four; a short hike to middle school, grades five and six; and an additional few blocks to junior high school. What can I say? It was a small town.

The home was huge compared to the apartment, with four bedrooms and one bath, but a little cramped for a single mom and two sons. I had my own bedroom and it was my sanctuary. I asked to have it painted dark blue. With the red carpet and white ceiling, it resembled an American flag in a box.

From this kid's perspective, the home had two really neat features, an attic and a basement. (I've lived in California for the past thirty-five years and haven't seen either in any home.) Even though the attic was cool, with its cedar closet and slanted ceilings—hiding a multitude of boxed treasures— my favorite part of the home was the partially completed basement. It had one of those old-fashioned furnaces; remember the one in *Home Alone* where Kevin (Macaulay Culkin) was afraid of the big, bad furnace when it kicked on? Me, too. I seldom ventured over to that side of the basement where the furnace lurked. The ceiling down there was about six and a half feet high, as I remember. I had a set of barbells and I couldn't do any exercises where I lifted them over my head—no space up above!

My grandparents had given us a small pinball machine, not the traditional big palooka with all the bells and whistles, but still pretty cool. I also had one of the first stationary bikes. It was the kind of bike you could crank down on the wheel to make the peddling harder and harder.

The former owner left an old wooden workbench along one wall. It was about eight feet long and had several drawers that were almost frozen shut with rusted age. I could see it in another time and place, a workbench filled with tools and gadgets, maybe leather goods being made. But our basement gave it another purpose.

On that bench, and as the centerpiece of the basement, stood a chemistry set. Those contraptions in the 1950s were big, sturdy, and intricate, not the small plastic ones you see advertised now. The cabinet was made out of steel, and as I unfolded the different sections, it spanned almost the entire eight feet of the bench. The various drawers housed mortar and pestle, tiny glass vials, and other tools of the trade. The accompanying book of directions gave young chemists like me the ability to put together various ingredients to make something uniquely different.

The set even came with a Bunsen burner to show you how heat could further alter those ingredients. How that house escaped my experimentation unscathed is a miracle in itself. I was always looking for ingredients I could combine to create an explosion, like with gunpowder. But even in the '50s, manufacturers had the sense not to include something that could blow up half the block.

Chemistry teaches that by adding different ingredients together, you get something unique. When hydrogen and oxygen are combined, either water or hydrogen peroxide results. Sodium and chlorine make salt. You get the idea.

I sometimes envision God using a heavenly version of a chemistry set to make unique human beings. It explains why each of us is different and distinct. Even identical twins have different likes and dislikes, different personalities, different hopes, dreams and talents.

Envision if you will, God at work, creating. He's got some sort of a vessel in which He adds the different fixings to make a person. First the basics. For instance, for me it would be: blond hair, blue eyes, fair skin, 6 feet in height, regular size feet and hands. Then the more intricate details, the nuances that make each of us distinct. He dips his hand into the vast choices of ingredients: a little dash of compassion, a modicum of musical talent, a pinch of artistic flare, a love of dogs, a dose of muscular coordination, a dab of the dramatic, an angelic vocal chord and a hint of empathy. Because He's got so many components to choose from, the combinations are limitless.

I like to think God uses his hands, rather than a scoop, a shovel, or a measuring spoon. It gives Him a much more personal, tactile feel for who we will become. And when He creates, some of his DNA rubs off on who He's making. You're made from his very hands; it's inevitable that some of Him is in each of us. The Bible declares that we are all made in His image; made literally by the very hands of God is one way to understand and visualize that.

Once He's finished, He admires his work. He knows it's the right formula, the perfect recipe. After all, He's God, so He doesn't make mistakes. He doesn't compare one creation with all his others. He's made the perfect you. Maybe not perfect to the outside world, but perfect to Him, to God.

I know He's got many creations to make, many people to craft, but I like to think He sits for a while to smile at you. For God, it's always about who you are, not what you do. He gave us free will so we will do what we will do—even if you believe that all we do is preordained and written in God's book. He loves you and showers you with grace and love—no matter what you do. So, the important thing to God is who you are, and since He built you to perfection, He sits and admires his creation.

He may have a template that He works from, or drawings, or a heavenly bill of lading with specific ingredients. Of course, He is God, so it might all be in his memory. If He intends to make an artist, He may refer back to his template of Michelangelo or Pablo Picasso. A scientist? Marie Curie or Copernicus. A musician? Maybe Stevie Wonder or Yo-Yo Ma. But then He goes off script, changing the makings and the mixture slightly. He doesn't make duplicates. Similar, but never an exact match. So to the template of John Lennon, He adds a little jazz and gets a John Mayer. To the template of your older brother or sister, He continues to tweak the formula until He gets you. Maybe He starts out with identical eye and hair color or the shape of the nose or jawline; then He gets creative because He doesn't work like those paint-by-number drawings we used as children. He doesn't need them. He has his own professional skills.

Then you are born. Perfect, whole and complete. Ready for the adventure—your life! I know that as we age imperfections appear for a host of reasons, but we didn't start out that way. We were built—handmade—with the heavenly chemistry set by the master chemist of the universe.

SCRIPTURE:

"I praise you because I am fearfully and wonderfully made; your works are wonderful, I know that full well."

—Psalm 139, v.14

"So God created man in his own image, in the image of God he created him; male and female he created them."

—Genesis 1:27

PRAYER:

Thank you master maker for creating me the exact way you envisioned. Thank you for all that I am and all that I will become. What an honor to be made in your image. Help me to live up to that standard. Help me to remember I was created by the Most High God, the maestro of creation. Reveal to me through your Holy Spirit what you want me to become in the world. Keep me on track and on purpose to fulfill the destiny that is engrained in my soul and speckled in my DNA. Help me to accept, embrace and love who I am. Keep me true to myself and your design for my life. Thank you, sweet Jesus. Amen.

Darra

I'd only known Darra a few short weeks before she died, but she taught me so much about life and love. Most of all, she taught me to let go of needing to know why everything in life unfolds the way it does.

When I was younger, I was very inquisitive. Not in all things, like science, for instance, because I don't really have a scientific mind. I could understand why the Earth rotates around the sun, why winter is colder than summer in the Northern Hemisphere (and vicey versy in the southern), but when it got to how the moon affects the tides, well, my inquisitiveness had its limits.

For the things that interested me, I have a very curious mind. I suppose I'm not too unusual in that regard. I wanted to know why the U.S.A. had a Civil War, so I bought a book that explained it in 100 pages. I wondered why Kerouac's *On the Road* was such an impactful book in its time, so I bought a copy. I've tried to finish it at least three times (I can't quite stay awake long enough), but I do understand on a deep-down level the need that Dean Moriarity and his peeps had to roam from coast to coast. And a curveball in baseball—how is it thrown and why does it curve? My son's coach showed me the basics. To better understand the workings of my wife's mind, I read a copy of *Men are from Mars, Women are from Venus*. I've learned a lot, but to say that I have that one figured out would be a gross overstatement and a stab in the heart to all men who struggle with that dilemma daily.

Then I met a young massage therapist in my late twenties. I hadn't had many massages in my life, but I was single, making pretty good money and putting my body through some grueling tennis workouts, so I signed up with her. About five or six massages into our relationship, I complained of a sore arch. I told her I'd been playing a lot of tennis, and a podiatrist had recommended an arch support for my flat feet.

She asked me if I trusted her. Not the usual diagnostic question, right?

I said, sure, as long as she didn't hurt me, I was a trusting soul. She told me she was going to ask my body why my arch hurt and that I should stay out of the conversation. *Say what?*

Don't ask how it works, she said, just trust me. So I relaxed with the warm towels and soft music, and she and my body got to talking.

She used a technique called muscle testing. After my body told her how to fix the pain in my arch, she worked her magic. I got up from the massage table an hour later and voilà, no more arch pain. It's never come back.

I've gotten more inquisitive with her over the years, and still see her occasionally, so I understand, somewhat, how she uses techniques outside the realm of modern medicine to heal. Her processes amaze me. I could write an entire book about that (and it's in the works, trust me), but that's a bit off subject here.

The point is, I've become more willing to accept what happens in my life without needing to know exactly why. I don't need to know how this computer mouse maneuvers the curser around this document, wirelessly, just that it works when I need it to. I don't think that makes me lazy or uninterested. I simply choose to spend my time not trying to figure everything out. That can reduce stress and make life flow more fluently. Sometimes you just have to accept what *is* and not get too bogged down with the *why*.

Now, back to Darra, who taught me a lot about that. That's her real name, and I'm sure she wouldn't mind my using it, especially if I say it's pronounced Dar' a, not Dare' a. (*Don't you dare call me Dare' a!* That's how I remember how to pronounce it; she would have never been so direct).

I met Darra on a Wednesday night. She was a pretty women, in her late thirties, but shy—timid, almost—and somewhat unsure of herself. I had arrived early at a new Bible study class at our church, and my job was to save a table for the 10 of us who met regularly to study the Bible, Jesus and life, not necessarily in that order. I was standing next to this empty table of ten chairs when Darra approached and asked if she could join me.

My usual response would have been no, I'm saving all these seats. But something in her eyes made me say yes. It wasn't quite desperation I saw. She looked a little scared, like she needed a friend.

We scrunched another chair around the table, and the eleven of us huddled close together over the next several weeks, enjoying a video series by Nicky Gumbel. It was a basic Christianity course, but Gumbel, a Brit, had a unique way of presenting it.

We learned that Darra had come to Christianity just a few days earlier, had a lot of questions, and definitely needed friends to help her understand her new faith. However, her family wasn't so sure about this religion, and she was getting pushback from her husband, who was a Jew. She'd broken from him and the Jewish faith, walked into our church, found a pastor, asked a ton of questions, and accepted Christ on the spot.

Over the next month, we found out what had attracted Darra to Christ. She had recently been treated for cancer—the serious, in your face, life-threatening kind—and had a desperate desire to know what follows death. I suspect many people teetering on the threshold of their last breath have the same questions. Is this all there is? What comes next?

The Gumbel course, along with her new friends, answered Darra's questions and assured her that a dedication to Jesus guarantees a seat on the flight to Heaven. To unbelieving souls, I've often said it this way: If you're right about life after death and I'm wrong, we both end up buried in a pine box in the ground. If I'm right and you're wrong, I end up in Heaven and you end up in Hell, which from my understanding is a whole lot worse than a pine box in the ground.

Then one week Darra didn't show up. When we called to check on her, we learned the cancer had returned with an unrelenting vengeance. A few weeks later she had passed on. We never saw her alive again.

We'd never met her husband or her two small children, but our group pitched in as much as we could for her funeral service. It was held at our church, and we helped with the wake in her home following the service. We ordered the food, served it, and cleaned up afterwards. We weren't there to answer faith questions or convert; we were there simply to honor our new friend and serve her family. No one asked us about Darra's new faith; most were too consumed with the shock of her sudden death. They only wanted to mourn and commiserate.

Darra taught me several lessons in the few months I knew her. Sometimes (not always, I regret), when somebody answers my question, "How are you?" I don't let them get away with a simple, "Fine, thanks." I look in their eyes, searching for fear or pain or confusion, or even desperation. Sometimes my reply is a simple, "Oh?" questioning their original response. It doesn't always work, and the atmosphere usually has to feel safe enough for them to dig deeper. It doesn't work too well if they're strangers, either.

Lesson #1: If you don't ask, you'll never know what people are feeling and struggling with in their daily life. And how can you *help* if you don't know?

I also learned that God puts people in our lives for many reasons—and you don't have to know why. It's like the moon and tides or the computer and the mouse. Quit trying to figure it all out and just love the person. I know, that's a heavy word. Love. How are you supposed to love somebody you met yesterday? Somebody like Darra? We couldn't cure her cancer, we couldn't heal her. We simply became her friends. We hugged her when we saw her, let her voice her fears and her tears, and served her however the moment led us.

Lesson #2: Open your heart for those dear souls that God puts in your path and do your best to love them. If you don't, you'll never know what you might miss. You could miss somebody like Darra, who in the few weeks she had left on this planet just needed a friend. *Be that friend.*

SCRIPTURE:

"The cords of death entangled me;
The torrents of destruction overwhelmed me.
The cords of the grave coiled around me;
The snares of death confronted me.
In my distress I called to the Lord;
I cried to my God for help.
From his temple he heard my voice:
My cry came before him, into his ears."

—Psalm 18:4-6

PRAYER:

Help me to trust you wholeheartedly, Lord God Almighty. Help me to love my neighbors, my acquaintances, and those I meet for the first time. Help me to recognize when others need a tender touch, a hug, or a soulful conversation. Open my eyes to those things in the world that really matter, and keep confusion or distraction for those that don't at bay. I confess, Lord, that I've missed those opportunities in the past, and I don't want to miss them again. Make me the kind of person who is touched by pain, moved by conflict, and convinced of your healing power. Thank you, sweet Jesus. Amen.

Eye for an Eye

A few days after the 9/11 terrorist attacks in New York City, my friend Dave and I lunched at a popular Mexican restaurant. But our mood wasn't festive. We both struggled with how to express our feelings about what had happened and were formulating what would be just retribution.

In my frustration, I blurted out, "Maybe we should just bomb the entire Middle East."

Dave looked at me in shock. "And kill millions of innocent people? That doesn't sound like a very Christian thing to do."

How right he was. My visceral need for justice—an eye for an eye—had lured me way off track.

It's one of the most famous yet most misunderstood phrases from the Bible: eye for eye, tooth for tooth. Old Testament stuff.

Exodus 21:22 includes a reference to men fighting and then hitting a pregnant woman; she then gives birth prematurely. As the chapter continues, we learn that if the woman experienced serious damage—I guess more serious than premature birth—the defending man can take "life for life, eye for eye, tooth for tooth…" (verse 24) and the list of retribution goes on from there.

In Leviticus 24:19-20, this command gets spelled out more clearly. "If anyone injures his neighbor, whatever he has done must be done to him: fracture for fracture, eye for eye, tooth for tooth. As he has injured the other, so he is to be injured."

I'm not exactly sure how they upheld this. If I knocked your tooth out in a fight, I wouldn't just stand there while you knocked out mine. Must have produced more than a few grudge matches.

In Deuteronomy 19:19-21, the phrase was used to deter more crime and violence. "…then do to him as he intended to do to his brother. You must purge the evil from among you. The rest of the people will hear of this and be afraid, and never again will such an evil thing be done among you. Show no pity: life for life, eye for eye, tooth for tooth, hand for hand, foot for foot."

Life for life. Pretty harsh, huh? The God of the Old Testament was a tough, old dude.

I suppose this is where the traditions of cutting off the hand of a thief and cutting out the tongue of a liar originated. Not to mention capital punishment. At some point in the history of man, everyone—or at least a majority—agreed that the punishment was just. Life for life.

The eye for eye equalizer might be harder to uphold. It's a bit nebulous. I mean, you wouldn't really cut out somebody's eye if they damaged yours, would you? What if you only "slightly" damaged their eye? You can see the problems arising, can't you? Even if eye for eye is symbolic—like tit for tat—the concept is hard to grasp.

But a life for a life is pretty clear. If you kill somebody, then you die. *"But I didn't mean to do it, the knife just slipped..."* isn't really a defense. Sorry, life for life; it's right there in the Bible, in all those places.

But wait, you didn't get the update? Bible 2.0? When Jesus came to Earth—part man, all God—he changed the rules. He updated the manual. He set in place a new covenant, a new testament.

From Mathew 5:38: "You have heard that it was said, 'Eye for eye, and tooth for tooth'. But I tell you, Do not resist an evil person. If someone strikes you on the right cheek, turn to him the other also. And if someone wants to sue you and take your tunic, let him have your cloak as well."

Game changer!

Don't get me started on all the lawyers and lawsuits, suing everyone for their tunics and cloaks. Let's save that for another day.

For now, let's talk capital punishment. At the time I write this, capital punishment has been banned in over 140 countries. From the list I found online there are several "civilized" countries that still allow it, including the United States, China, Japan, Taiwan and India. I'm not saying the other 140 countries are uncivilized, but they are not the world's leading countries—make no mistake about that—in size or influence.

In the U.S., the death penalty is legal in only 22 states. In California, where I live, the death penalty is well...dying a slow death. After being reinstated in 1978, 13 people have been executed at a cost of over $4 billion. It costs much more money to house an inmate on death row, even if they are eventually executed, than if they are confined to life in prison. All the mandatory appeals involved in death penalty cases drive the price skyward. So, please, don't tell me that it costs so much to house these murderers for life. No, it doesn't. It costs way more to try and kill them.

Recently I saw that the state legislature in Utah was debating the return of the firing squad. Seems lethal injection was not so humane—it took too long and made the victim suffer needlessly. So now the state of Utah—Utah, being one of the more "religious" states in our Union—is considering using marksmen to aim for the heart. What's next? Hanging by the neck until dead? Good grief.

Haven't we all seen stories in the news lately of convicted criminals set free because new DNA technology proved their innocence? Some of those innocent criminals had been convicted of murder. Could it be possible that somebody who has already been executed had been innocent? Not just possible, but probable. If it's happened only once, once is one too many times.

Why are we clinging to capital punishment? I don't know. I've never had anybody in my family—or anyone I've ever known of—murdered. Maybe I would feel differently if I had. Maybe I'd want 'eye for eye, life for life'. I don't think so though, and I hope I never have to consider that question. I know I'd find it almost impossible to forgive someone who murdered a member of my family. Forget what the Bible says about forgiveness. C'mon, you think it would be easy to forgive? No way.

Okay, what about justice? Would it be justice to me personally to have somebody killed that murdered a member of my family? I'd want justice for sure, but I'm not sure I would want that person executed. I think if the murderer got life in prison without the possibility of ever being free again, that would be justice enough for me. But again, I'm hoping I'm never in a position to have to make that determination.

Remember those plastic wristbands that have the initials WWJD? What Would Jesus Do? They were supposed to be reminders to make us behave like Jesus would in any given circumstance. I never wore one, but I understood the concept.

What would Jesus do about capital punishment? What would He say about the death penalty?

He might say, *"You who are without sin, cast the first stone,"* or in this scenario, *"flip the first switch."*

But some people would counter with, "I'm not a murderer so I'm not a sinner in that regard, and I'll flip that flipping switch!"

Then Jesus might say, *"Who are you to judge? To take a life? Only God can be the final judge of life and death."*

But again, I know people who don't believe in God or Jesus, and they may point out that there was a judge in the courtroom and twelve people in the jury box.

How do you convince somebody who doesn't know Christ that Christ *wouldn't* kill people? That He would forgive them, like all the people in the Bible He forgave. I almost wish there was a story in the Bible about how He forgave a murderer. It would make it easier to make the point. But even so, I still know some Christians that I can't convince to give up their conviction to the death penalty.

The website Red Letter Christians writes eloquently about the evil of seeking justice through torture and execution. You may want to surf over to their site to read and absorb their reflections of the sanctity of human life.

Recent polling shows that Americans are increasingly opposed to the death penalty. I suppose it will continue in the U.S. for a time, and gradually fade away into history. At least I hope so. I know that the opposition fluctuates; as the crime rate goes up, Americans tend to support the death penalty more. If terrorism continues to escalate, there may come a time when a terrorist will be on trial after killing many Americans—many more than the Boston Marathon bomber—and we'll have a tough time not demanding a "life for life" (or "lives").

But maybe we can simply silence our hearts in prayer for those killed and their families in mourning. Maybe we can continue to develop a system of justice that doesn't bring more darkness and death to the world.

Commandment #6: You shall not murder. Most all of us would say that we can keep that commandment. But I think it means more than simply refraining from the act of murder. I think it means to cherish the opposite of murder, to cherish life. All life, everywhere, on God's planet.

Now, I can pray. I can pray for compassion. And I can write. I can write with compassion. I just hope in the meantime that more innocent people are not put to death for crimes they didn't commit. Good grief.

Thanks, Dave, for getting me back on track. Next time, lunch is on me.

SCRIPTURE:

"But love your enemies, do good to them, and lend to them without expecting to get anything back. Then your reward will be great, and you will be sons of the Most High, because he is kind to the ungrateful and wicked. Be merciful, just as your Father is merciful. Do not judge, and you will not be judged. Do not condemn, and you will not be condemned. Forgive, and you will be forgiven."

—Luke 6:35-37

PRAYER:

Oh, Heavenly Father, show me the way. Make my path clear. Let me feel your heart, let me feel your compassion, let me feel your love. Sometimes I can't feel my own heart. I have no compassion, and I have no love. I know that's not you. I know that's not the Holy Spirit in me. I know that's wrong, but I can't help it. I want justice, I want redemption, I want revenge. But I also know it's not *mine* to want. You are my guide. You live in me. Help me to tap into you, help me to feel like you, and to love like you. Help me to be strong under harsh criticism or in the midst of toughened and hurting hearts. Make me bold, make me compassionate, make me *love*. Thank you, sweet Jesus. Amen.

Bobby Knight

Bobby Knight slowly sauntered out to midcourt, got right up in my grill and looked me in the eye. "I think I'll call you Susie from now on. You are such a little girl. YOU'RE AFRAID TO GET YOUR KNEES DIRTY!"

I could smell his breath as spittle hit me in the face as he yelled at me.

Knight is one of the most successful college basketball coaches of all time. His teams won over 900 games before he retired. He was a demanding, demeaning and some say demented coach, throwing chairs, hitting players and occasionally acting like a spoiled two year old.

He was also a jerk.

Maybe *jerk* is too strong a word. How about verbally abusive? At least I can attest to that.

I was a high school basketball player and our head coach sponsored a coach's clinic one Saturday. Local coaches would come and listen to other coaches discuss strategy and tactics. The star attraction that day was Knight. Everybody wanted to see his practice drills and techniques, and how they were led to so many victories. His nickname in later years was "The General" though I'm not exactly sure why. Maybe it was because he loved to send his troops into battle.

The high school players demonstrated the drills. Knight selected me and another player to participate in one special "battle". We all felt a little apprehensive doing drills we'd never seen before. Some of the coaches that day were good teachers; Knight taught through abusive intimidation.

My teammate and I were standing underneath a basket, looking toward the other end of the basketball court. On each side of the court were two additional baskets. They folded down from the ceiling and made courts that ran perpendicular to the main court, so we could see six baskets in all.

Knight held the basketball. In rapid fire, he designated a color to each basket. This one is white, that one black, blue, green, red, and yellow. As soon as he finished, I had no idea which basket was which color. He then explained that he was going to roll the ball toward midcourt. When he blew his whistle, we were both to run out toward the ball. When one player commanded the ball—*commanded?*—then Knight would call out a color, and the two players would play one-on-one to that basket. Got it? No, not really.

He rolled the ball slowly. He blew his whistle.

I ran out, beating the other player by several steps, leaned down and scooped up the ball. Okay, I was thinking…which basket was what color?

Then the whistle blew again. "Stop, stop, stop!" he boomed.

Knight sauntered out, and that's when he started to call me Susie. He shouted at me, "Now do it again, and this time I want you to fight for the ball like two men, not sissy little girls!"

I didn't think it was a good time to mention that I beat the other kid to the ball by six steps.

We lined up again. He rolled the ball. He blew his whistle. The two of us immediately started punching each other, and as we reached the ball, we dove. I won the battle and commanded it.

Knight called out a color.

I took off for the nearest basket, thinking he probably didn't remember his intricate color scheme, either.

He blew his whistle again, ending the drill, and looking toward the crowd of coaches. "That's how you teach that drill!"

He called me Susie the rest of the day. I take back my earlier statement. He *was* a jerk.

Do you look at God in a similar way? In your view, is He demanding, unrelenting, over the top, or in your face?

He certainly appears to be many times in the Old Testament, doesn't He? Right from the get go, Eve plucks a tiny, red apple and she banishes all women to an eternity of heavy-duty pain in childbirth. And poor old Adam gets a life of working in the dirt. Both are kicked out of the nicest, coolest place ever created, the Garden of Eden.

And God's hits just keep on coming. Even before you can blink your eyes, God is so frustrated with the whole human race that He commands Noah to get the ark ready. You probably know the rest of that story—it doesn't end well for humankind. Before we finish the first book of the Bible, Genesis, God has destroyed two complete towns because the townsfolk were way off track.

You could read the rest of the Old Testament and easily come to the conclusion that God gets mad at His people and continues to command, reprimand and punish them. He's trying to keep them in line with a heavy hand, a quick temper and deadly results.

But I like to think of the Old Testament as a story of God creating this perfect spot—this garden paradise—for man and woman, and they keep soiling the place with trash and garbage.

God tries to correct their habits, they don't change, He gets ticked off and sends a little Hell on Earth down their way. But He always forgives them, gives them another chance, they muck it up, and the whole process repeats itself.

God has one more idea, His ace in the hole, to finally get man and woman back to the garden. As a heavenly spirit, God can't quite move the earthlings to get with the program. Follow me and I'll take care of you. Do what I say, and don't worry, I've got your back. Keep my commands, and you will have everything you need.

Uh, no thanks, we said; we'd rather do it our way. But thanks for the tips, much appreciated. Buh-bye.

I can almost picture God saying to himself: what did I just hear? How in the world can I get it through their thick skulls? I tried all the miracles—manna from Heaven, parting of the Red Sea—those didn't work. I tried all the great men—Moses, Isaac, Abraham, David—they had their successes but in the end, we're back at square one. I even tried showing up personally on occasion—the burning bush, the cloud in the sky. But nothing. Are they really that thick they don't get it? I suppose I'll just have to go down there myself—in human form—and try the kinder, gentler approach. Let them see me die for my people. That'll turn their heads and hearts back to me.

Enter the Christ.

Isn't it interesting that God came as a little baby? Sure, it was a miraculous birth considering His mama was a virgin. But still, God is God, and He could have come back as a young man. The Bible doesn't record much of Jesus' early life before His ministry started at age thirty. Why didn't God just start there? Maybe to the Jews it was important to fulfill all the prophesies of His birth, but to most of us, the reason for Jesus is *why He came* and what He gave up to save us.

I suspect God needed to be a complete human man, from birth to death. Do not pass the terrible twos, potty training, acne, and adolescence. Experience it all, the good and the bad. Then we can get down to business.

Jesus didn't wipe out men like God had done earlier. He raised them up from the dead. Jesus didn't drown the entire race with a worldwide flood. He offered them living water. He didn't turn men or women into pillars of salt. He proclaimed they would be the salt and light of the world. He didn't promote strong men to rule over His kingdom, like Samson and David. He blessed the meek men and told them they'd inherit the planet. He didn't praise the warriors who fought in the name of God. He gave praise to the peacemakers and beckoned to them as His children. He didn't even say "an eye for an eye." No, He turned his other cheek and said I'll take another.

The God of the Old Testament is the history of God. The God of the New Testament is today's God. Loving, helpful, always willing to listen. Sure, He has a few rules, but they aren't the 600-plus laws God gave the Israelites. *Jesus doesn't lay down the law, He lays on the love.* And that's all He asks of you. Just love me back—I'll take it from there. Love your neighbors, too, while you're at it. What could it hurt?

Jesus doesn't get in your face or on your back. He'll never call you Susie, unless of course, that's your name and what you prefer. He's there when you need Him, but if you say you don't need Him… Well, He's got an awfully full schedule, so that's pretty much your call.

The Garden is still open for business, by the way. Jesus maintains it now, in all its splendor. And I hear the apples are out of this world, like nothing you've ever tasted—to die for!

SCRIPTURE:

"Oh, Jerusalem, Jerusalem, you who kill the prophets and stone those sent to you, how often I have longed to gather your children together, as a hen gathers her chicks under her wings, but you were not willing! Look, your house is left to you desolate. I tell you, you will not see me again until you say, 'Blessed is he who comes in the name of the Lord.' "

—Luke 13:34-35

PRAYER:

I love you, Jesus. I love everything about you. You are an awesome father to me. You never scold or punish me. You love me no matter what I do. You are so full of grace. I know you promise you'll never leave me or forsake me. I'm so sorry I forget that sometimes. Keep reminding me, heavenly Father, that you were sent to love me and I was built to love you back. Help me to love myself; help me to love my neighbors, even if they're basketball coaches that might need a little love themselves. Thank you, sweet Jesus. Amen.

490

It started out innocently enough, as most things do. But it ran dangerously off the rails and required a huge helping of forgiveness before the episode ended.

An email ignited it—an email from my old girlfriend:

> *Hi, how ya doin'? Haven't heard from you in a long time. Everything okay on your end?*

You can see the first red flag, can't you?

Me? I missed it. Totally.

At the time, my wife and I had two young kids. Active, involved, busy, crazy kids that demanded a lot of attention. My back bedroom business was starting to take off, and I spent a lot of time planning and creating, selling and delivering services. When I sold one, I delivered it and then I was on to selling and trying to deliver the next one. It was stressful, because even though I was my own boss and it was exactly what I wanted to do, the business was demanding. Life was full and exciting and hectic. Sometimes when couples hit that stretch in the road, their relationship can take a backseat to the demands of life, especially to kids and jobs.

Losing focus on the marriage because of life's demands can open you up to temptation. So can rough patches. If you're married, you know the kind. As a couple you don't always see eye-to-eye on things. You disagree, you discuss, sometimes heatedly, maybe even vehemently. If you're lucky, you back off to your respective corners, not wanting to push your side too hard, out of respect. But something lingers—like the smell of last night's meal still in the kitchen. You believe you were right; or you think the other person didn't understand or respect your opinion. Maybe conversation between you two falters for a while. Since you don't exactly know how to talk about what's bugging you, you don't talk much at all. You know you'll both come out of this eventually, you just don't know when that will happen. And sometimes when you're in the middle of that rough patch, something else pops up to distract you.

Like an email from an old girlfriend.

My wife and I began our Christian journey during those hectic days of a new business and young kids. We'd joined a church, attended a Sunday class to learn more, and became really engaged in the process. But we didn't know much about prayer and the discipline of asking Christ for help every day. We absorbed everything we could, but we hadn't been engaged in the spiritual journey long enough to fit all the pieces of the puzzle together. We were still learning the story of the Bible and the impact Christ could have on our lives, but we didn't have much practical application.

Then the next email arrived.

Hey, I'm going to be in your neck of the woods next month.

Uh, oh.

Wanna try and get together?

This time I saw the red flag, bright and flashing in front of me, waving like a matador's cape in front of a frantic bull. And I ran right *toward it* instead of away from it.

Then it got worse. How could it get any worse? Oh, it's not that hard to figure out, is it? I did what any stupid, clueless, idiot husband would do. I lied.

"Hey, hon, I'm thinking of going up to the city next weekend. An old college friend will be in town."

Technically, that wasn't a lie. She *was* an old college friend, an old college *girl*friend. I just left out that one, tiny four-letter word detail. Oh, the tangled webs we weave. That old girlfriend was bringing her girlfriend with her, so it was innocent enough. No chance of getting into too much trouble there, right?

Wrong.

I went. We caught up with each other. And nothing happened. Until I got home that evening.

I confessed. At least, that's the way my warped brain remembers it. Probably what really happened was that my wife smelled a rat—*me*. And she asked me, in her polite yet direct way, what had happened. She wanted the details. I cracked under the pressure. Under the deceit is more like it.

I'd hurt my wife. Deeply. Not just the visit, not just the lie, but the combination of everything. We didn't kiss goodnight that evening, unlike every other night since we'd been married.

But she forgave me.

Oh, not right away. I didn't deserve "right away" forgiveness. She also didn't let me forget about the whole incident. She's smarter than that. Every once in a while, the subject happened to come up. A little poke from her, about the "old girlfriend" dinner. I'd apologize again. It wasn't a one-apology offense. Probably at least a seven-apology offense, maybe more.

Then, one day, several months later, I realized we'd gotten through the rough patch. No more pokes, no more apologies. Forgiven completely. Let's not bring it up again. Whew! Fine by me. Off the hook, but I was changed for the better.

By definition, grace is forgiveness when it's not deserved. I've known wives who have forgiven their husbands for much worse. I applaud those women.

But not as much as I applaud my wife. In our thirty-one years of marriage, I've done way more than my share of the apologizing. Because I've also done way more that I needed to apologize for. With my wife, there is no limit to her grace. There is no overload, no point when she stops forgiving. I keep apologizing, she keeps forgiving. I suspect in the next thirty-one years, the scorecard is going to show similar results. However, she doesn't keep score. She's that kind of woman. I know. I'm lucky. Blessed even.

Now is the time in the story that I reveal the moral. Actually, I've got a few. We'll number them, so they'll be easier to remember.

1. Don't answer emails from old girlfriends (or old boyfriends).
2. Watch out for those red flags.
3. Don't lie to your wife (or your husband).
4. Beg for forgiveness, if you missed any of the first three.

But you know it's not that easy, don't you? Please tell me you do. Sure, we can learn from our mistakes. I've made the same mistake more than once in my life. (No, not old girlfriend mistakes. I'm not quite that stupid). But still, isn't that the definition of being human? That we make mistakes? Okay, it's not the scientific definition, but it fits, right?

We all get distracted. Life can be tough at times. It can come at you like a locomotive. A locomotive in disguise—like an old girlfriend, or boyfriend, or a get rich quick deal, or a too-good-to-be-true sure thing, or a little white lie, or a big hairy bodacious lie that grew out of a little white lie, or a flirty smile from a co-worker, or a I-won't-get-caught, or a it's-not-that-big-of-a-deal… Stop me when you get the point.

This isn't a story about morals or distractions. It's really a story about forgiveness. It wasn't easy for my wife to forgive me. After all, she's only human.

But Christ *isn't* human. He's God. It's easy for Him to forgive. It's His nature. And He tells us to forgive others as He forgives us. He instructs us to forgive seven times seventy. That's 490 times. That's a lot of forgiveness. Let's hope none of us would ever need that much.

There's no such limit for Christ though. He'd go way past that 490 marker. So you can never do anything so evil, so heinous, so stupid that He wouldn't forgive you. Isn't that inspiring? Doesn't that lift a huge weight off your shoulders? If you're so deep in the lies, secrets and deceit that you think nobody will ever forgive, guess what? Christ does. Just fess up.

Your guilt might not leave you right away. Maybe that's okay; you might need to suffer a bit with it, to make it sink in, to see the error of your ways, but it'll leave eventually. And you'll come through it a better person. A person who will be able to forgive others as you've been forgiven.

I don't know how many of those 490 chits I've used up with my wife. I'd hate to guess. Maybe 30? Higher—50, 60? It's possible. I've been married a long time and as we've already established, I'm a ridiculously slow learner and I slant significantly to the stupid side. I'm just glad I married the woman I did. Thanks, hon. In case you need to hear it again.

SCRIPTURE:

"Count yourself lucky, how happy you must be—
>   you get a fresh start,
>   your slate's wiped clean.
Count yourself lucky—
>   God holds nothing against you
>   and you're holding nothing back from him.
When I kept it all inside,
>   my bones turned to powder,
>   my words became daylong groans.
The pressure never let up;
>   all the juices of my life dried up.
Then I let it all out;
>   I said, "I'll make a clean breast of my failures to God."
Suddenly the pressure was gone—
>   my guilt dissolved,
>   my sin disappeared."

—Psalm 32, The Message

PRAYER:

I make mistakes, Lord. I lie, cheat, steal, and do them all again. I can't help it. I'm weak, I'm miserable. Help me, Father. Search my heart and my tongue and my mind, and keep them clean. Watch me. Don't take your eyes off me, even for a second. Keep distractions at a distance; don't let them near me. Help me confess—to all that need to hear it, and especially to you. Wipe my slate clean. Forgive me, again...and again...and again. Thank you, sweet Jesus. Amen.

Cowboys

I love Saturdays. Who doesn't? Even when I had to work weekends as a young man, Saturdays held a special allure. I suppose it goes back to school days when Monday through Friday were days you had to go to school, and Sunday was the day you had to go to church *and* the day before the five days you had to go to school. But Saturday was your day, no encumbrances, no dread, your free day to do with what you wanted. Fridays were a close second, because the excitement of the next day was palpable.

As I kid I never slept late on Saturdays, even if I had stayed up late the night before watching horror movies, which in my neck of the woods always played at 11:30 Friday night.

When we were young boys, my brother and I would get up early on Saturday mornings, make ourselves cereal and settle in front of the television. TV in the 1950s was in its infancy and Saturday mornings were full of either cartoons made in the '40s or cowboy movies of the '30s and '40s. We had our favorite cartoons, that's for sure. (Anybody remember "Clutch Cargo"? Didn't think so). But we were cowboy fans through and through.

We could watch two or three movies on a Saturday morning. Each spanned about sixty minutes, including commercials. One of our favorites was Roy Rogers. We liked him better than Gene Autry, although their movies were almost interchangeable. Each had a special horse and a comedic sidekick, and both sang. In later movies, Roy had a wife, Dale, and Gene usually featured a heroine or love interest, too.

But our choices weren't limited to Gene and Roy. The list of cowboy heroes generated by Hollywood in that era was endless. Many were "B westerns" meaning not quite A-quality work. Some stars transitioned to A-list movie stars, including John Wayne, Randolph Scott and Joel McCrea. Starting with the early stars, Ken Maynard, Buck Jones, Tom Mix and progressing through some of the last western movie stars, like Rex Allen, "Wild Bill" Elliott and Guy Madison.

Our personal favorites included:
John Wayne

Johnny Mack Brown
Randolph Scott
Joel McCrea
Hoot Gibson
Tex Ritter
Tim Holt
Lash LaRue
Tim McCoy

I still watch westerns today. Encore, a cable TV network has a channel that runs westerns all day every day, including old western TV series. I've watched so many westerns in my time, I'm embarrassed to admit that I even know the real names of many of the "bad guys."

But why the allure of westerns, and old ones to boot? I think it's because I can tell the good guys from the bad guys. I'm not sold on the idea that the good guy always wore the white hat and the bad guy the black, but in many reels, that was true. The good guy usually rode the white horse, too.

The second fascination of western movies was the happy ending—I always knew the good guy was going to win. Even in the rare case where the bad guys won, like the latter day *Butch Cassidy and the Sundance Kid*, they were likable rogues who didn't do anything all *that* bad.

For the most part, the good guys won because they faced up to the bad guys. They took a stand at the crucial time in the movie and if they had to fight, they fought. They fought for truth, justice and what was right.

Today, the lines between good and bad are blurred, if not downright indecipherable. In Josh McDowell's classic book, *Right from Wrong*, published in 1994, his vast study revealed that today's youth have a hard time telling, well, right from wrong. At alarming rates, lying, cheating, physical abuse, illegal drug use have become everyday features of that generation's youth. And that was a generation ago. Do you think it's gotten any better? Probably not, and maybe, it's worse.

While in his late teens, my son often said, "Well, Dad, that might be okay for you, but it doesn't work for me."

What he was saying was: It might be right [or wrong] for you Dad, but those are your old-fashioned codes and morals, not mine. Where did he get those ideas? From society, from friends, from movies, from parents who don't teach right vs. wrong, from schools where kids' self-esteem is more important than teaching right and wrong, and yes, from me, who isn't perfect and makes his share of mistakes.

God has some rules that are black and white, no gray area. Ten such rules are called the Ten Commandments. Some are easy to follow, such as *don't kill*.

Some are easy to ignore, like don't covet your neighbor's wife. Hey, what's a little lust between friends? *I'd never really come on to her. I'd just lust after her over the back fence. What could that hurt?*

And some are a little murky these days. "Don't give false testimony" and "Do not steal" —in other words, don't lie or cheat—but fudging on your taxes, ingesting illegal steroids to up your game, or hiding income in offshore accounts are actions often admired by some segments of society.

And besides, didn't Jesus come to rid us of all that old law in the Old Testament? Rules and law led to self-righteousness, but not to loving others.

I don't envy kids these days—or parents. You used to know that a skirt above the knee was wrong to wear in polite society. Now short shorts above the…well, you know…is perfectly acceptable. Many schools cannot even enforce dress code rules for fear of running into legalistic parents hell-bent on upholding their kids "right to free speech." Talk about throwing the baby out with the bathwater.

Right and wrong—it's not so easy to define in all cases these days, is it? Abortion for some people, especially of the Christian faith, seems wrong. But what about the woman victimized by rape or incest? War and killing people, is wrong; but what about the humans victimized by tyrants or lunatics? Could anyone question going to war to rid the world of Hitler and his Nazi regime? Illegal drugs are well, illegal, so, therefore, wrong. But states have said that even if marijuana is wrong at a national level, it's right in Colorado and Washington. So is it right or wrong? Depends on where you live!

When I was growing up, it was illegal for blacks to drink out of the same water fountain as whites. And homosexuality was buried really deep in the closet. We've come a long way, baby, and we will continue along that spectrum—maybe kicking and screaming—until we get it right.

So, the question of wrong or right might depend on *when* you lived, too, not just where.

So much criticism today aimed at Christianity results from Christians coming off judgmental, and so critical of other people. "I'm holier than thou, 'cause I don't do the horrible things you do." Really? C'mon. We all live in a fallen world, and none of us measure up. We all fall way short of Christ's standard. Some days I can't even repent, I'm so far away from Him. To criticize others when I'm such a scumbag seems pretty hypocritical to me. Maybe even it's the definition of hypocrisy.

Ah, there's the dilemma. We still need to operate and exist in a world that deciphers right from wrong, don't we? If we tend to go on our own way—to ignore all the rules—then even traffic would stop. If people didn't obey traffic signals and laws, we would all be in deep doo-doo.

I've tried to say my standard is Christ; if it's wrong for Him, it's wrong for me (and society). That worked on my kids when they were young, but as they got older I got the same reply: He is for you but He isn't for me. He may be your standard, Dad, but not mine.

So sometimes, I fall back on my heroes of yesteryear. I stand tall when I have to. I face the bad guys, sometimes only when I have to, or I'm forced to. I fight if I have to. Not with my fists, but sometimes with my voice or my pocketbook. I love my wife and I do my best to let her and my kids know it. I love my kids unconditionally; they're adults now and they don't need me lecturing them. I might not have been a perfect parent, but they know right from wrong. I take action against things I believe are wrong. I stand up for things I think are right. I really don't care what others think of me and I won't let them dictate to me what they think I should believe.

At the end of many western movies, the cowboy rides off into the sunset. He's done his job; he was a hero for 60 minutes. The townsfolk have come around to understand that his fight was worth it, whatever the sacrifice. Even though Christ is still my standard and my ultimate hero, I have several cowboy hats in my office to help me understand that in everyday life, we still need cowboys; we still need the good guys.

SCRIPTURE:

"The law of the Lord is perfect,
reviving the soul.
The statues of the Lord are trustworthy,
making wise the simple.
The precepts of the Lord are right,
giving joy to the heart.
The commands of the Lord are radiant,
giving light to the eyes.
The fear of the Lord is pure,
enduring forever.
The ordinances of the Lord are sure and altogether righteous."

—Psalm 19:7-9

PRAYER:

Thank you, Lord, for teaching me right from wrong. Your Word guides and instructs me. Give me the will to read it and the mettle to see it through in my life. Remind me to call on the Holy Spirit to help me. Let me be humble,

Jesus, when faced with my own righteousness. Keep hypocrisy away from my door. Help me find ways to convey your standard to an unbelieving, fallen world, so that I don't come off as "holier than thou" to others. When I see wrong in the world, Lord, help me to fight. Give me the courage to combat evil, to take a stand against what you and I know must be fought. Provide me the words and the actions to be a hero when you need one. Thank you, sweet Jesus. Amen.

The Joy Choice

When I mention my first book to friends, a novel I wrote called *Hard Left*, some people ask if an e-book edition is available. For a long time I said no, only the print book, because I prefer a paper copy. I realize it's probably an old-fashioned, archaic way to look at things—not considering what others desire. But it's hard to know what others want or need. Sometimes I don't even know what *I* want or need.

After my family and I moved out of one house and into another, my viewpoint changed. Since we were leaving a home we'd been living in for fifteen years, we had a yard sale where I tried to sell a few books I'd owned for many years. Nobody wanted to buy them. Okay, I understand. A biography of Wilt Chamberlain is probably a little out of date. Then, I tried to donate the books to the library. They said they had quite enough old and not-too-rare titles, thank you very much. In fact, the library had a bookrack on the way out the door with free books. *Take my books, please.* It was always full. I was tempted to slip *Wilt the Stilt* in there to see if anybody took it, but they had rules about dropping off unsolicited books.

These days, I don't buy every book I want to read like I used to. Now I buy maybe five a year, ones I know I'll want to keep and maybe reread. Of the other 30 or so books I read every year, I get the rest at the library. Since I write fiction, too, I peruse the section of new books there and often look for debut novels. They give me hope that someday, one of my novels will be published. (I independently published *Hard Left*). I can also evaluate how good my first novel is compared to others. That kind of assessment is hard to do sometimes only because I believe some sections of my book are brilliant! But then again, I'm just a wee bit biased. Of course, there are sections I would give anything—like tickets to see Elton John in Las Vegas—to rewrite, too.

On occasion, I find a first novel that is so uninteresting, I want to do anything else but read it, even listen to rap music or drink my wife's cucumber shakes. Then I find a jewel. A book so enthralling I know I'm incapable of ever writing even one sentence that would be on par with that entire book.

I also enjoy browsing in the religion section of the library. During my morning reading time, I often find myself needing enlightenment. I do my best to read from the Bible each morning, but I also crave contemporary commentary about life and God. Sometimes the Bible can be confusing. I'm reading Revelations now. Go ahead, read a chapter of that book, any chapter, and tell me exactly what it means. I'll wait.

I thought so. Couldn't do it, could you? (Well, maybe you could; you're probably a lot smarter than me.)

The other day while I was browsing in the library's religion section I found a book entitled *A Thousand Names for Joy: Living in Harmony with the Way Things Are.* I don't always live in harmony, so that book beckoned me. Once I got it home, I found that's it not at all about God. The nice thing about borrowing books from the library is that you can return them unread. I won't tell and nobody will know.

But it still beckoned, so I read the first eight chapters or so. The preface states that the book is author Byron Katie's response to the Tao Te Ching, which is "the great Chinese classic that has been called the wisest book ever written." I think I have a copy of the Tao someplace, probably in storage, but I'm having trouble reading Katie's response, so I'm not sure reading the Chinese version would be much help. I know, I know. It's translated, but still.

The title sums up the gist of the book, but there's a paragraph from chapter three, describing a scene where the author is preparing a salad. Then the phone rings and as she walks to answer it, she trips and falls. She then explains how the floor was just doing its job, just being there, and how it must have been time for a little rest. Since she ended up on the floor. She definitely has a knack for accepting whatever comes her way.

I'm not sure I would have let the floor off so easy, but that's just me. We have wood floors in the home we live in; maybe Ms. Katie has plush carpeting. I suspect the point is: *live in the now, accept and embrace what is, move on.* I wanted to ask the author what about the welt on her head or the chipped tooth when she became one with the floor, but later in the book she writes about how there is no actual pain in the world, so I'm not sure she'd be open to that question.

I do admire her ability to stay in the moment and experience joy in everything. Joy has been a top-of-the-mind topic for me for nearly a decade. It started in a Bible study group I was attending when the leader noticed I wasn't joyful a lot. Like almost never.

She asked me why not? After all, she said, I was a chosen Son of God. He promised He would never give me more than I could handle, and said that if I came to Him and asked for anything, He would always provide. And to top it off, I was guaranteed a position alongside Him in heaven for eternity. What was there *not* to be joyful about?

Of course, another group member pointed out that the Bible also says this life will be full of trials, we live in a fallen world, the devil is always lurking and no matter how hard we try, we are sinful people. Touché.

Webster defines joy as great happiness or pleasure. My thesaurus gives me matching words like gratification, satisfaction, contentment, enjoyment, gladness, delight, elation, rapture (probably not the Jesus kind) and bliss. But those seem to be emotions, and emotions come and go.

Henri Nouwen describes life as moments when joy and sadness kiss. There's always joy, there's always sadness, and at any moment, they both exist in your life. They are like two hands coming together—in a handshake, a clap, a prayer.

I could fill you up with Bible verses about joy. Here, try these: Isaiah 12:3, 1 Peter: 8-9, Matthew 5:1-12, Luke 15, John 13:1-17, Galatians 5:16-26, Philippians 4:4-9, John 15:1…the list goes on and on. But no matter how much the Bible teaches us that we should be joyful, sometimes it's just plain hard to do that. I'm not the type of person who wakes up joyful and stays in that state of mind throughout the day, no matter what.

There are probably humans out there that are like that. Joel Osteen comes to mind. Have you ever seen that guy *not* smiling? I love to read his books, especially when I need a boost. Here are a couple of his gems:

"Don't magnify your problems. Magnify your God. The bigger we make our God, the smaller our problems become."

"We must stop cursing the darkness. Let's start commanding the light to come."

He's all about the positive: positive outlook, self-talk, self-image, thoughts, words, vision, and future. Okay, you get it. Dwell in joy—ooh, I like that. Dwell in joy. But almost every time I dwell there, I slip. It seems I cannot dwell too long. So how do I prevent myself from slipping from joy to darkness? My Bible study group pondered this question and came up with individual ideas: prayer, adoration, sharing, and listening.

I think you also have to notice the traps that keep you from dwelling in joy. Some of my traps are idolatry (money, sex, grief…money, sex…). I lose sight of joy and fall into the trap. Sometimes, I don't even know I'm in the trap. Sort of like the frog who is put into a pan of water, and the water is gradually heated until the frog dies. He never thinks about jumping out because he doesn't notice the incrementally rising heat. It probably feels like a nice, warm bath for a while.

Oh, I know, you were looking for the definitive answer here, weren't you? But there might not be one. I can use music or riding my bike or a great draft ale to jerk me out of my funk. You have your go-to funkbusters, too, I bet. My wife does yoga, which is somewhere about #49 on my funkbuster list.

But you already know the answer, don't you? This is not rocket science. Ready? Dwell in joy. Choose joy.

Simple. And not so simple at the same time. It is your choice.

Scripture:

"Be joyful in hope, patient in affliction, faithful in prayer."

—Romans 12:12

PRAYER:

Thank you, heavenly Father, that you choose me; that you died for me; that you gave your Spirit to guide me. Thank you for allowing me to be a child of the Most High God. Thank you that you know me, cherish me and love me. Keep me in your word, in your life, and in your world. Turn my eyes from darkness to the light. Keep that villain Satan away, keep temptation away, keep my idols locked up and chained down. Help me to see you. Help me to see your light. Help me to see the joy I have in you. Help me to dwell in joy. Thank you, sweet Jesus. Amen.

My Two Dads

My father was brilliant, especially in science and math. I remember spending many an evening at the kitchen counter as he taught me long division, fractions, geometry, algebra, trigonometry, and calculus. Well, actually, I don't remember that he taught me much about calculus. All of us have our limits, and with calculus, I hit the wall.

He attended an Ivy League college, Brown University, and studied chemistry. The actual story of why my father left Brown and joined the Navy is a little murky. My brother and I speculate that he may have been asked to leave, but nobody in the family has ever talked about it.

When he returned from his World War II tour of duty in the Pacific, he finished college in our hometown at a small, liberal arts school and immediately entered the family business—selling cars. A bit far removed from chemistry, isn't it?

Later in life, he drank too much. Maybe my father was drowning in the pain of dreams lost, of what might have been had he completed his studies at Brown and found his calling in molecules instead of motors. I'm not sure.

My father-in-law was brilliant, too. Of German descent, he grew up as part of the first generation in his family born in the United States. His parents directed his studies toward medicine. As he used to tell the story, they practically demanded that he become a doctor. But he always wanted to be a teacher. After college, his own WW II tour, and medical school, he set up a family practice in Cincinnati, Ohio, his hometown. After twenty years as a successful general practitioner, he decided to follow his original dream. He and my mother-in-law took time off to tour the country and eventually settled in California, where he accepted a job teaching at a medical school. Perfect. For the next thirty years he pursued that dream, combining his love of medicine with his desire to teach.

I rarely saw my father-in-law have a second beer or glass of wine; one was usually his limit. He was one of the most genial, gentle, fun and happy men I've ever met in my life. He always seemed so *content*.

My dad in contrast, was bold in business, using his street smarts to the best of his ability. He had great intuition about the automobile business, made strategic decisions to capture market share, was fair but never let anyone take advantage of him, and passed along a thriving enterprise to my brother, who took over the family jewel as the third generation in the business. He never once talked about missing an opportunity in life, usually had a great attitude about living life on your own terms and always encouraged me to follow my dreams.

He took me to church as a young boy, but for my sake, not his. He suffered from cancer, and near his death, I told him I was praying for him. He told me he never believed too much in that kind of thing. I don't see how he could have spent all those Sundays in church without some of the gospel rubbing off on him. I got to tell him I loved him many times before he died, and even though we struggled at times with our relationship, I still miss him today.

My dad-in-law used his love of medicine and teaching to carve out a unique career. He invested his money wisely and always provided well for his family. Maybe he saw where medicine was headed in this country—where family doctors spend almost as much time with insurance companies as with patients—and found a better way to pursue his teaching dream and still contribute to the future of medicine instructing new doctors. His son observed his legacy, the caring he exhibited to everyone, and followed in his father's footsteps to become a doctor.

My dad-in-law and I never spoke about religion or Jesus. I know he and my mom-in-law attended church regularly, especially after he retired, and like many in that generation, faith was in the fabric of their upbringing. He died a decade ago, in his sleep, and I still miss him today.

A tale of two fathers. Similar in many ways, yet so different.

Sometime you get lucky in life and can follow your dream. Right from the get-go, things just seem to fall into place. You get the right education. You are surrounded by great mentors. You have the abilities, demeanor, and fortitude to pursue your destiny. The pieces of the life puzzle seem to almost arrange themselves and a crystal clarity guides you along the path that is so natural, so right. Life ordains.

But sometimes, life sneaks up on you and you make the best out of it. Life happens and it can feel like you have no control. War breaks out and you're called to serve. People die and you have to step in and be the breadwinner, maybe before you're ready. Babies are born, unexpectedly, and life takes a hard left. You find your balance, eventually. You absorb the blow, whether glancing or a direct hit, and stay on your feet. You may stagger a bit, but you don't let yourself get knocked down. You not only survive, you thrive. Life happens.

Sometimes you find the courage to change your life and make it better. Following the prescribed path is easy for some. Others sense a different way, off the beaten path, forging a new trail, even if it's new only for them. Maybe you have to backtrack to find a new beginning—a cut in salary, a return to school, starting over again at the bottom. But that sense, that feeling, that gut instinct, is a powerful lure. It calls your name and you can't resist. You suck it up, muster the nerve, get your game face on and jump in, head first. There is no holding you back. Life beckons.

I loved and admired my fathers, but I'm puzzled by both of them. Were they simply unable to talk about their faith? Or were they still searching for faith? Did they know Jesus, or did they know only the church? We all know and admire people—strong, confident, uplifting people—but we don't know anything about their faith because they didn't, or couldn't, or wouldn't vocalize it.

Sometimes Jesus is nowhere to be found. He's left the building. It seems like He was never there at all. But wait? You attended church as a child. Your parents made you go. There was that scripture, in a framed needlepoint, hanging in the dining room. Your friends took you to vacation Bible school that one summer. Your grandmother watched Robert Schuller on TV all those Sunday mornings. You listened without saying a word when your college professor debated why "In God We Trust" shouldn't be on our national currency. You prayed before dinner, maybe the same prayer every single night for years. You recited, *"Now I lay me down to sleep... "* as a child, even if the part about dying before you wake creeped you out.

You need to know that sometimes Jesus is just in the fabric of life. In the woodwork. On the other side of the door. Sometimes Jesus rubs off on you. You didn't want anything to do with Him, but He was there, He was around. You pushed Him away; He took a step back but He never left. You directed the movie of your life and He wasn't a cast member. But He never left the movie set. He took a bit part, an extra, maybe in the crowd scene.

Life can work with Jesus as a bit player. I don't necessarily recommend it, but let's be realistic, it happens.

You don't have to preach Jesus; you just have to practice what He preaches.

If you struggle with the whole religion thing—and don't we all at times—then focus on Jesus. If church isn't for you, then find another way to get to know Jesus. If the Bible is a little too difficult to decipher, and yes, it definitely can be, then read *other* books written about Jesus or God. That's how I discovered that sometimes Jesus can appear how you least expect Him to, even dressed like a lumberjack.

And if life moves just fine for you, whether it's in the direction you want it to go or the direction it simply must go, take heart. Jesus is still around, still available. He may be in the back of the theater watching your movie or brushing up on the one line in the script that He gets to say as a walk-on. But He's there. He's always in the fabric of life, in the woodwork, ready for action.

I hope both my dads knew Jesus personally and accepted Him as their savior. The Bible says only that guarantees a spot in heaven. When my dad was dying of cancer, I was a Christian newbie, only a few years into my journey. I didn't have enough faith in my faith. I hadn't met the lumberjack yet or seen the real power of the cross. I let Dad slip away without telling him my story, Christ's glory, God's plan for salvation.

I'm sorry, Dad. I let you down; I wasn't strong enough. I hope beyond all hope that by some miraculous divine deathbed intervention you made it to Heaven. You, too, dad-in-law.

I miss you both.

SCRIPTURE:

"Do you not know?
Have you not heard?
The Lord is the everlasting God,
the creator of the ends of the earth.
He will not grow tired or weary,
and his understanding no one can fathom.
He gives strength to the weary
and increases the power of the weak.
Even youths grow tired and weary,
and young men stumble and fall;
But those who hope in the Lord
will renew their strength.
They will soar on wings like eagles;
they will run and not grow weary,
they will walk and not be faint."

—Isaiah 40:28-31

PRAYER:

I want to do this on my own, Lord. I don't want your help. It's important to me to prove that I can do it. Please let me try. Okay, then, how about if you just stay close. Within earshot, within the sound of my voice, my whisper. Look over my shoulder. Direct my hand or my word or my thought. Sometimes I feel so far away from you, like you were never even there. But I know you're close by. I sense it, somehow. I go off in my own direction without any concern for you at all. Reel me in, bring me back, turn me around. Calm me down and straighten me out. Let me breathe you in; let me get you into my lungs. Linger inside me, Lord. Thank you, sweet Jesus. Amen.

Love/Hate Haiti

My wife had this great idea that we should spend our twenty-fifth wedding anniversary in Italy. It wasn't my first choice, but I've learned to trust my wife immensely, especially when it comes to discovering the world.

I can't remember why we didn't actually go to Italy until about six months after our anniversary. We planned to arrive in February, which we knew might be chilly, but since we could save a little money during off-peak season, we booked it.

After we finalized our itinerary, we found out that our daughter had missed the deadline to study abroad during the fall semester of her senior year in college. She did manage to secure a spot in a program in Spain starting in January. You see where this is headed, don't you?

The phone call soon followed. "Hey," she said, "you guys are going to be in Europe the same time as me. Why don't I come to Italy, and we can tour together? I have a week off, and we could even fly to Barcelona, too."

Uh-huh, nothing better than sharing a dinky hotel room during your epic romantic anniversary trip to Europe—with your daughter!

My daughter had been in European time zones for a month by the time we arrived, and she had traveled during her weekends all over Europe. She was in this "I've got to see it all while I'm here" mode. She wanted to get up at 7 a.m. every morning—about the same time that my body was finally going to sleep. She also liked to walk at a four-minute-a-mile pace everywhere she went, so she could see more things. Somehow, she never got tired, ever, probably because she was twenty years old. Which was thirty-eight years younger than her jet-lagged, sleep-deprived father, who had gotten about twelve minutes of sleep the night before.

It was a great time; my wife has photos to prove it.

When I finally got my phone working, about midway through the second week we were there, I found a voicemail message. It was from the CEO of a non-profit on whose board of directors I sit. He said he had just gotten back from Haiti; he wanted to start another non-profit, and he wanted to buy 100 percent of my time for the next three or four months. At the time I was a consultant, selling my time to clients, and to a consultant, he spoke the magic words. I called him from Barcelona, and we set up a meeting for the day after I got back.

So began my love/hate relationship with Haiti.

The CEO's vision was to help rebuild Haiti after the devastating earthquake of January 2010. Anywhere from 100,000 to 300,000 people had died (there's some controversy about the actual number), over one million people were left homeless, and 27 of 28 government buildings in the capital city of Port-au-Price were leveled, leaving a government that barely functioned before the quake virtually helpless.

My job—my paying job—was to do all the communications for the new company. Things like come up with a name, website, logo, business cards, marketing materials, etc. The first project for Extollo International (Latin for "raise up") was to rebuild an orphanage housing 50 girls in Leogane, the epicenter of the shaker. These 50 young ladies, ages one to twenty, lived in a single room with no electricity, no indoor plumbing, and no kitchen. They made meals over a fire outside, used an outhouse, and luckily had a well on the property. But to get water, they had to haul it up with a rope and a coffee can.

During the year-long construction of a brand new orphanage—with indoor bathrooms, showers, septic system, rain capture tanks, and electric lights and ceiling fans—we discovered that we couldn't find any local Haitian men or women to help us build. There were few trained construction craftsmen in Haiti; reconstruction utilized the same methods that caused everything to collapse in the first place.

Here are a few sobering facts about Haiti you might not know:

- It's the poorest nation in the Western Hemisphere.
- Less than 2 percent of its population earns a high school diploma.
- School is not free in Haiti, so many Haitians don't attend at all or only complete a few grades.
- Unemployment hovers between 65-70 percent.

So we tweaked our business plan. We added training in construction skills for Haitians into our building projects. We began with the basics—this is how you hold and swing a hammer. Yes, very basic. Then we built curriculum, but found even though it was translated into Haitian Creole, some of our trainees couldn't read. (See bullets above.)

It was still a really good gig for me. The CEO of this new company was paying my monthly invoices—out of his own pocket. This took place after the recession that devastated my consulting business, so I kept sending the invoices.

Then I went to Haiti.

My home church had donated some money so that I could buy new beds, mattresses and sheets for the orphanage. My first two days I spent with a guide touring the Port-au-Prince area looking for those supplies. This was a year after the quake and the capital was still barely functioning. Stoplights were out, stop signs non-existent. Roads were so bad, you had to hang on inside the car because you were getting tossed around so much. The air stunk—with dust, debris, excrement, spoiled food, and so much else it was hard to determine what it was.

People lined the streets. Some were afraid to be in their homes. Some had no homes. Some were selling whatever they could get their hands on to make enough money to buy food for the day. I saw one tall, elegant Haitian man by the side of the road. He'd made a roadside stand out of a few big rocks and a long wooden board connecting them. On the board stood 6 quarts of motor oil and beside it lay 4 huge, used truck tires. That's what he had; if he sold anything, he might eat that day. If not, he probably wouldn't.

When I returned after that second day to the makeshift shelter on the grounds of the orphanage, I cried. Tears flowed, no stopping them. I cried for the way people were living, I cried that it looked like they would live like that for a long time. And I cried because it seemed at the time that whatever I did couldn't make much difference.

When I got home after ten days in Haiti, I never sent the CEO another invoice. I joined the board of directors and dug in to make a difference. I had a cause bigger than my consulting business. I had seen God's suffering children in Haiti, and it broke my heart.

Sometimes I want to go back to Europe and lounge on the Amalfi Coast and sip Italian wine and wait for my daily gelato. I don't want to think about Haiti's poor, its plight, its future. We've been in Haiti six years now, and although it's better—everything is better—it still has a long, long, long way to go.

Funny thing is, once your heart is broken, it doesn't heal. It's not like a broken bone in your body. Sometimes when you break a bone, it actually grows back stronger than before. But once you witness firsthand God's children suffering, you can't forget them. You can try to ignore them, but once God convinces you that His people need your help, then go ahead, I dare you, try your best to ignore God.

It's hard to do. Almost impossible. If you do, you feel like Hell, literally.

For me, I got to a point in my life where I couldn't ignore God anymore. My consulting business faded away. The need to make more money slipped from my everyday consciousness. The need to prove myself, applaud myself, and promote myself vanished.

So why did I call it a love/hate relationship with Haiti? I love that now I work to improve what has broken the heart of my Lord. But I hate that I can't make a bigger difference. I love myself and what I've become when I work for the people of Haiti. I hate that I don't do it better or more often. I love the people of Haiti and I hate the way life has turned out for them. I love the orphans of Haiti and how they latched on to me, how they stroked the hair on my arms and the blond hair on my head; how they always ended up in my lap, needing and craving a simple human touch. I hate that there are so many of them, abandoned. I love that my heart's been broken, but I hate that I still try to forget I know it has been. I love Haiti and hate myself for still wanting to forget it.

SCRIPTURE:

"Then the Lord reached out his hand and touched my mouth and said to me, 'Now, I have put my words in your mouth. See, today I appoint you over nations and kingdoms to uproot and tear down, to destroy and overthrow, to build and to plant.' "

—Jeremiah 1:9

PRAYER:

Show me, heavenly Father, those things in the world that break your heart. Let my heart be broken, too. Help me take a stand to do what I'm able to do. Keep my heart tender and touched; don't let me lose that compassion you've given me, Lord. Don't let me forget, even if I beg you to. Don't let me get away with a half-hearted effort. Continue to work in me, be in me, and guide me to those people in your world that need me. Give me your Spirit daily as a reminder. Keep me tender-hearted, Lord. Thank you sweet Jesus. Amen.

Big Time Wrestling

At the junior high school I attended in Pennsylvania, physical education teachers would make the boys wrestle once a year for a couple of days. All part of a well-rounded PE education, I suppose. I never much enjoyed getting up close and personal with a stinky, sweaty pubescent young boy—not my idea of a good time.

Give me Big Time Wrestling any day.

For those of you who missed the heyday of wrestling on television—the 1950s and 1960s—let's revisit those glory days of yesteryear.

Wrestling on TV back then was live theater at its best. You had plot lines, good guys and bad guys, suspense and intrigue and lots of good quality, fun entertainment. Oh yeah, and a little bit of actual wrestling. (Most of it was fake.)

My favorite wrestler of the era was Bobo Brazil. Bobo's real name was Houston Harris, and if you look him up today, he gets credit for breaking down the color lines in wrestling, like Jackie Robinson did in baseball. A large, overpowering black man standing 6'7" and weighing 270 pounds, Brazil played the hero in most matches. Often pitted against such villains as The Sheik, Dick the Bruiser and Gorilla Monsoon, Bobo used his famous Coco-butt, head-butt and pile driver techniques to pull out victory when all looked lost.

The beauty of wrestling was that the show producers let the villains win occasionally so you'd tune in next week to see them get their just rewards. This back and forth between hero and villain continued week to week, leading up to the championships. Sprinkled into each week's hour-long matches, tag-team bouts pitted two villains against two heroes. The bad guys were not beyond cheating, usually just out of sight of an unsuspecting stooge of a referee, often throwing the hero out of the ring and hitting him with a metal chair. No kidding. It was great fun, especially since you knew all the headlocks, body blows and chair bashings were all part of the act. The brutality was a put-on.

This type of wrestling is still around today and continues to draw big crowds to live events like WrestleMania. The wrestlers these days might be jacked up on steroids, buffed to the max, and masterful at taking the spectacle to new highs—or lows depending upon your openness to this type of entertainment. Wrestlers of days gone by weren't in such great shape and didn't spend as much time in front of the camera, but they still delivered a great show.

Of course, boxing was popular back then, too, much more popular than today. "Friday Night Fights" aired every week on TV. Even though boxing went through a period when its legitimacy was questioned with accusations that boxers threw or "fixed" fights, the brutality of the sport could never be doubted. The objective in boxing is to hurt the other guy. Not many sports claim that dubious distinction.

Now we have the MMA. Mixed martial arts. How in the world did we progress from the fake head-butt to the legitimate chokehold?

MMA and all of its iterations have amped up the brutality to a new level. Wrestling is held in rings surrounded by rubber band-like ropes. You can always escape by slipping through and pleading, "no more, no more," as the crowd jeers. MMA is in a steel cage—no escape and no quarter given.

In wrestling, the objective is to "pin" the opponent's shoulders to the mat. The wrestler can always opt out of a more painful technique—like the camel clutch, the sleeper hold or the chinlock—by slapping the mat and forfeiting the match. In MMA, one way to win the match—other than beating the living snot out of your opponent—is to choke them. They can "tap out" before they black out.

In wrestling, illegal maneuvers like hair pulling, eye gouging and stomach punching happened just out of sight of the feckless ref. In MMA, you can openly punch, kick, and maim to the cheers of the adoring crowd.

What's next in spectator sports? Dueling pistols at 20 paces?

Does it say something about our society when the games we watch take on such a brutal nature? Certainly fantasy movie serials like *The Hunger Games* depict a futuristic fascination with a duel-to-the-death mentality. Even today's NFL football, arguably our nation's most popular sport, produces stronger, faster and more violent players. The serious consequences of such violence, such as concussions, make us all hesitate, doesn't it? Shouldn't it?

I like the gentler sports. I enjoy baseball, for instance. So much so, I'll watch it on TV, attend major league games, and even go to local college or high school slugfests. Many people say baseball is too slow for them.

I enjoy watching tennis. But I admit, I liked it better when John McEnroe and Jimmy Connors dueled. They spiced that gentleman's game up a bit. Most people say tennis is too tame and takes too long.

I like bike racing. On TV that is. Professional bicycle racing is probably the world's worst live spectator sport. OK, here they come! Swoosh, they're gone, buh-bye. Gone in sixty seconds.

I would never say to you, don't watch boxing on TV or don't go to a live bout. I would never tell you to give up MMA or other such brutal sports. I would never try to make you stop watching football; I enjoy it myself. And I don't mean to suggest that all those participants should relinquish their dreams. I know that some kids see boxing or fighting or football as a way out of poverty, as a way up to respectability, as a way to make a decent living. And I wouldn't deny them that.

Playing sports teaches many great lessons to our kids. This isn't a dissertation about learning to play fair, accepting defeat gracefully, or sacrificing all for victory. It's about exploring where we draw the line.

Are we going to continue to push our young boys into the combat of crippling sports? And, don't get me started on our young girls. Does anyone really want to see women boxing or punching and kicking each other in MMA? Some may, but for me, that's over the edge.

I know, I'm hypocritical. My son played high school football and earned a scholarship to play on a college gridiron. He was lucky—only one operation on his ankle, a broken hand, and several minor injuries. He made it out alive, and we're hoping that over the course of the next fifty or sixty years none of those injuries come back to bite him.

If my son were entering high school right now and asked to play football, I might try to talk him out of it. I could make a decent argument, pointing out all the news in the NFL of concussions, memory loss, debilitating injuries and even suicide brought about from brain damage.

I admit that I don't know the solution. The money to be made in most of these sports is too big, the stakes too high. We're probably down the road too far to give it all up or even change it much. But I have hope. Soccer has finally gained a foothold in this country. Lacrosse is exploding in popularity. Even basketball has lost none of its allure among our youth.

And I know not all kids play sports. Some play music, some write poetry, some sing and dance on stage. Good for them.

My son just had his first son. Both of my grandson's parents love sports, as do their extended families. Chances are the young boy will be athletic, maybe even gifted like his daddy. And I don't really want to be the grandpa that recommends he take up archery or competitive dance.

I've been trying to tap into Jesus on this one, too. I suspect He'd say He has other more pressing things to work on. Maybe He'd suggest that we try to be a little bit gentler with everyone, including our enemies or opponents.

I suspect I'll just keep on praying that we tone things down a bit. That in a sports-crazed society we can teach our children to enjoy the tender things in life, too. That we work with our coaches, especially at the youth level, so they're a little less concerned with winning at all costs. That we look after our athletes better and change the rules to keep them safer. It's time we care enough for people to let at least some of the money go.

Where's Bobo Brazil when we really need him?

SCRIPTURE:

"Blessed are the poor in spirit,
for theirs is the kingdom of heaven.
Blessed are those who mourn,
for they will be comforted.
Blessed are the meek,
for they will inherit the earth.
Blessed are those who hunger and thirst for righteousness,
for they will be filled.
Blessed are the merciful,
for they will be shown mercy.
Blessed are the pure in heart,
for they will see God.
Blessed are the peacemakers,
for they will be called sons of God.
Blessed are those who are persecuted because of righteousness,
for theirs is the kingdom of heaven."

—Matthew 5:3-10

PRAYER:

Sometimes, heavenly Father, I don't even know how to pray. Sometimes I merely look to you. I seek your face; I seek your council. I reach out in knowing nothing and plead that you'll guide and direct me. Take me where you want me to be, Father. Show me the way. Show me *your* way. Help me to be bold, changed, different than everything and everybody around me when I need to be. Give me your strength and your courage. Prepare me, equip me, teach me. Thank you, sweet Jesus. Amen.

Restaurant Critic

My workday in San Francisco had ended successfully. Excited and pumped, I was ready for a night in The City, as the locals call it. And although my dinner plans had fallen through, San Francisco offered a ton of choices to a young man like me with money in his pocket and vitality flowing through his veins.

Then I saw him. A young man, under thirty I guessed, but with a weariness in his bloodshot eyes. I'd spent many days and evenings in the city by the bay, mostly working, but often having fun. Every time I went there, I saw them, the homeless. But this time was different.

Approaching me with a smile as I exited the downtown San Francisco hotel at dinnertime, he sidled up beside me, like an old friend or colleague would do. As I walked down the street, he walked with me. He was engaging, a good conversationalist, and dressed better than most of the street people I'd encountered. Black pants, black coat, and white shirt—maybe his only decent outfit, his Sunday best—though they were a bit tattered, as if he'd slept in them the night before. (He probably had.) His hair was messy and a little greasy, and the man needed a shave, but he didn't smell bad. Many of them do; most smell like urine or sweat stink or both. But I knew his end game—he wanted money.

At first, he acted like a prospective tour guide. *What brings you to The City? Here on work or for pleasure? Are you getting to see all the sights?* Then he shifted to a restaurant critic. And let me tell you, there are no shortages of restaurant critics in San Francisco. Everybody has their favorite three or four, and they don't mind telling you about them. Of course, he shared his favorite. *Heading to dinner? Where are you going? Need me to make a recommendation? I love that little diner on the corner up there.*

He'd stopped walking, so I did, too. I knew I should just keep going, just walk away from him. Maybe he wouldn't follow. But he was so engaging. He turned around and pointed to that diner a block away. I knew the place. It wasn't fancy or expensive, by San Francisco standards. It featured a lunch counter in its center with individual swivel stools and red vinyl booths all along the windows facing the street.

Then came his pitch. I knew it was coming, but he'd built up the suspense so well that I had to stick around just to hear it.

"Listen," he said. "I don't want your money. I'm hungry. Why don't we just go up to that diner? You have to eat anyways. You can just buy me dinner. That wouldn't be so bad, would it?"

No, it wouldn't be all that bad. I didn't have dinner plans, but I really didn't want to spend time with him. He probably didn't want to eat with me, either. He probably wanted me to slip him a twenty, tell him to have a nice dinner, and walk away.

I walked away. He was disappointed, I could see, but his eyes quickly shifted to his next target. The next possible meal ticket.

It wouldn't have hurt me to slip him the twenty; I could afford it. But I'd been programmed to be wary of street people. *He'll probably just buy a cheap bottle of wine or something.* But he didn't look like a drunk. He looked hungry. *Maybe he needs a fix; maybe he's a druggie.* I suppose he could have been; life on the street can be hard and a little toke might make it feel a tiny bit better. *Maybe he'll get aggressive; maybe he'll try to rob me.* But he hadn't even touched me, always smiling, always polite. *Why doesn't he just get a job like the rest of us? He's certainly capable of finding work, isn't he?* But he *was* working—he was panhandling. It's a job for some folks.

Ever heard of the broken windows theory? It says that if a window is broken and left unrepaired in small towns or large cities, that makes passersby think that nobody in the city cares and nobody is in charge. In other words, minor, seemingly insignificant quality-of-life crimes, like throwing a rock through a window, could lead to more violent crime. I'm not saying the theory is true, because it is controversial. Critics say it leads to Gestapo-type police forces that arrest everyone for every little thing, like littering or jaywalking.

Sometimes the homeless problem gets tossed in with all those broken windows. Cities can't figure out how to solve the problem, so they make panhandling or loitering a petty crime, trying to clean up their cities by clearing out their streets. But homelessness isn't a crime, is it?

I don't claim to have the solutions to all the world's problems; sorry, I'm not smart enough to write that book. I'm just trying to keep my eyes open to pain and suffering in the world—and help you see it, too.

For instance, take a look at my buddy. He was my best friend for a number of years in Los Angeles. Always fun to be around, he laughed a lot. He could engage you in a great conversation, but he could also lead you astray pretty quickly. He liked to smoke a little weed (okay, a *lot* of weed), and he liked to snort a little coke. (No, *not* a lot; he couldn't afford it.)

He got so distracted by his guilty pleasures that he lost a few jobs. This was a pattern in his life; he liked to have fun way more than he liked to work. When he lost the last one, the economy was bad, and he couldn't find another. At some point, his wife had had it up to here, or maybe past here. She gave him an ultimatum: get a job, keep a job, or get out.

He'd burned too many bridges, and jobs were hard to find. I'd moved away from LA during all this, though I'd stayed in touch (not like a best friend would, more like a distance relative). I'd had to distance myself from him, too. Temptation was too great for him, and it was rubbing off on me.

Then he called one day, and I could feel the fear in his voice. He'd lost his joie de vive, his panache. Ultimatum day was fast approaching. He had no job, no prospects, and no money. He was a step away from living on the streets. I'd already loaned him money, and I figured the request was coming in again. But the line went silent. He didn't ask, just groaned, barely audible, like a tiny terror escaping his lips before he could stop it.

Without even asking my wife, I offered our back bedroom to him. He could stay as long as he had to. He was overtaken with emotion; he never expected me to make that offer. It never crossed his mind. *Really? What kind of a best friend was I that he didn't even expect that from me?*

He never took me up on the offer. Not long after that phone call he found a job, reconciled with his wife, rejoined his family. A step away from the gutter, he'd recovered his stride just in time.

Maybe his wife's ultimatum pushed him to the edge of that gutter. I suspect she knew he wouldn't fall into it. Maybe my offer helped rescue him from that ledge. He'd needed to know somebody cared enough to offer a hand to steady him, to help him avoid the fall.

Maybe my buddy wasn't so different from the guy in San Francisco, my tour guide and restaurant critic. Maybe that guy had just lost his job or been issued an ultimatum from his wife. Maybe he was down on his luck or had lost his stride, and ventured too close to the edge. He probably wasn't a drunk or a druggie. Maybe he just needed to know somebody cared. Now I wished I'd slipped him that twenty.

Why are we so afraid of the homeless? So what if they trick us with a let's-get-dinner scheme? I can afford a buck, or a five, or even a twenty, can't you?

A church in my hometown offers the homeless a shower. They have a portable unit with just enough water and privacy—and everyone leaves with a set of clean clothes. Another ministry in the Bay Area motors around in a mobile home, equipped with shampoo stations and foot washing tubs—and offers a clean pair of socks and a slightly used pair of shoes. Neither solves the homeless situation, but both help in a unique, caring way.

I could see Jesus and His followers doing either one of those, couldn't you?

One of my favorite pastors in the world has this great idea to help people show that you care. Stop by a fast food restaurant and buy a bunch of gift certificates, in five-dollar increments. The next time you encounter somebody who needs a handout or a hand up, offer them one or two.

You don't have to fix every broken window in every town. You just need to show one person at a time who is close to the edge or over the edge that somebody cares.

SCRIPTURE:

"Then Jesus said to his host, 'When you give a luncheon or dinner, do not invite your friends, your brothers or relative, or your rich neighbors; if you do, they may invite you back and so you will be repaid. But when you give a banquet, invite the poor, the crippled, the lame, the blind, and you will be blessed. Although they cannot repay you, you will be repaid at the resurrection of the righteous.' "

—Luke 14:12-14

PRAYER:

Don't let me turn away, Lord. Help me to see my brother and my sister. Let me be a little gullible, a soft touch. Soften my heart so that I can feel another's pain, another's suffering. Help me from becoming so jaded, so fearful, so much a skeptic that I can't see through your eyes, heavenly Father. Give me your sight, so that I might see. Give me your heart so that I might feel. Give me your hands so that I might reach out. Thank you, sweet Jesus. Amen.

Suffering

One third of Americans support a family of 4 on less than $44,000 a year. A quarter of Americans do it for less than $22,000 a year—that's called the poverty line. In 2010, over 20 million people in the United States lived in extreme poverty, earning below $9,000 a year for a family of 3. We were still in the throes of the Great Recession so maybe that number is smaller now, but maybe not. And that's in the U.S., the richest country in the world, by some standards. Think what it must be in Haiti, or India, or Guatemala.

Half of the jobs in America pay less than $34,000 a year. Half. A quarter of the jobs in America pay less than $22,000—the poverty line. A quarter.

Welfare rolls in the U.S. have shrunk dramatically since 1996, from a high of over 14 million to about 5 million. Although the number of families receiving food stamps has increased, we still have around 6 million Americans whose only income are food stamps—they have no jobs, no income, no Social Security, nothing except food stamps. That's 2 percent of Americans, 1 in 50.

Most people think that people of color dominate poverty in America. And although it's true poverty is disproportionately present among African Americans and Hispanics, the largest number of poor people in the U.S. are and always have been white.

In the U.S., about 80 percent of kids graduate from high school. That doesn't sound too bad—after all, in Haiti the number is less than 2 percent—until you understand that those who don't graduate are more inclined to spend time in the juvenile justice system, or prison, and traditionally stay in low-paying jobs for their lifetimes.

The statistics aren't great elsewhere, when you look at households headed by a single parent, the growth of female-led households, the rising number of people incarcerated (disproportionately people of color), and the gap in wealth from our richest citizens, the 1 percent as they've been labeled lately, and the other 99 percent.

Any discussion of poverty in this country, along with its related issues—education, jobs, income gaps, and more—is a complex undertaking. If some of these statistics raise questions or concerns or outrage within you, good. Maybe you need to dig deeper. This essay isn't meant to offer solutions, but rather, point to an issue. The issue of suffering. It's not only prevalent in third world countries. This kind of suffering occurs in the U.S., too.

I don't know squat about suffering. Sometimes when I read about it or see it first hand, I need to suffer a bit myself. To actually feel it physically. To make it real for me. To try to understand it better.

I have it really good in life, there's no denying that. I have a college degree, a track record of good paying jobs, money in the bank; some would say lots of money in the bank. I eat 3 full meals a day, usually every single day, and I have a refrigerator full of food. I even have a mini-fridge in the garage for the overload. When I feel over-privileged or when I overindulge, or when I face the facts that there are *way* more people in the world who have it so much worse than I do, I need to suffer.

For instance, I've fasted many times. My longest fast has been four days with only juice and water. (The pastor at our church went forty days that time, so I'm very humbled by my measly four.) Let me tell you, at first it hurts. Physically. My fasts have been based on the idea that if I deprive myself of food, I do it as a sacrifice. I don't do it to cleanse my body or rid it of toxins. I don't do it at Lent, in repentance of a particular something I did that I want to atone for. I do it because I want to.

However, I don't feel I fast often enough. I used to do it once a week, but even then, I'd only fast two meals. I'd eat a big dinner the night before, fast for breakfast and lunch the next day and try not to eat before din-din rolled around again. Big whoop, huh?

Sometimes I make myself suffer on my bicycle. It's a purposeful way to suffer because I usually feel too good or too blessed or just too lucky in life. I get on my bike and I ride. And ride. And ride till it hurts. Eventually if I ride hard enough and long enough, it will really hurt. And then I'll want to get off or call Uber for a ride home. But I don't. I keep going so I can suffer.

I don't mean I go for a leisurely bike ride, slapping on suntan lotion, turning my ball cap on backwards and hiking up my board shorts. No, I strap on my spandex uniform with the micro fabric, padded shorts, my high tech helmet, my reinforced bicycle shoes and my $100 biking sunglasses and hit the road. (Hey, if I'm going to suffer, at least I'll suffer in comfort.) I don't suffer much before the 20-mile mark unless I'm really going balls to the wall. So I push further.

These suffering rides are not fun rides—they are meant to hurt. They are not meant to get me into better shape—they are meant to shape me into a different person. They are not meant to build my cardiovascular endurance—they are meant to soften my heart for others.

Some people sell all their possessions and move to the mission field. They live in remote villages somewhere in the world and help the less fortunate. They sacrifice everything and suffer immeasurably to be there. That's not me. I wish that it were; I wish that I was built that way. To put my wants and needs aside and just give everything to those who need it more. But I'm too set in my ways, too attached to the comfort in my life for that.

I can go through a few arduous hours on my bike until it hurts or I can deprive myself of food and drink for a couple of days. I can spend a week in the mission field, no problem. But that's just sporadic suffering.

Most of us don't know real suffering. The kind where you wake up every day to nothing, the kind that lasts all day and will be there again tomorrow. Sure, we've suffered through periods in our life—broken relationships, heartache, divorce, injury, abuse, sickness, death of a loved one—when it feels like life is unfair, or cruel, or unbearable. But we all come out the other side. Maybe we've learned something about ourselves or others that makes us better, stronger. We'd have rather not learned the lesson the hard way, but we suspect it's better than not to have learned it at all.

Most of us know how Christ suffered for us. We know all the ways He suffered—forty days in the desert, praying so hard for us that He bled, battling against all evil, the cross, crucifixion, extreme pain, and then death. He suffered it all so we would have a path back to God. So we wouldn't *have* to suffer.

We're not meant to live a life of suffering. We are destined to live a life of grace, and faith, and love.

But we have to suffer so we can see suffering. So we can recognize it. So we can fight it. So we can remedy it.

If you are suffering and it seems like you've been there forever, take heart. God wants better for you. He wants to heal you, He wants to restore you. He wants to restore your marriage or restore your health. He wants to restore your joy and give you the peace and happiness you've only ever dreamed about having. He doesn't want just a period of restoration; He wants a lifetime of restoration for you. He wants to restore your relationship with God, the Father. For an eternity.

If you're suffering, take heart.

If you're not, take notice. Maybe suffer a little bit yourself. That might be all it takes for you to be part of the solution.

SCRIPTURE:

"Rescue the perishing;
  don't hesitate to step in and help.
If you say, "Hey, that's none of my business,"
  will that get you off the hook?
Someone is watching you closely, you know—
  Someone not impressed with weak excuses."

—Proverbs 24:25, The Message

PRAYER:

Help me to understand suffering, Lord. Make me aware; don't let me hide my eyes; don't let me shield my heart. If I need to suffer, heavenly Father, I'll do it. For you and for your people. I know you don't want me to have a life of pain, of sorrow, of misery. I believe you have a better life planned for me— and for your children. Open my eyes and break my heart for those around me that cannot see, that cannot hope, that find it hard to believe. Give me courage and strength to witness everything in life. Give me boldness to step into the fray. Give me your light to shine in the darkness. Give me spirit to feel, love to heal, life for eternity. Thank you sweet Jesus. Amen.

Letting Go

That particular August day in Central California emerged hot, oppressively so. The college campus was deserted, simmering in the sun with a sense of lethargy; summer school was winding down and fall classes at the university didn't start until late September.

My son had earned a college scholarship to play football, and today was the day his mother and I delivered him to school. I would say "dropped him off," but that would mean we were picking him back up. Deep in my heart, I knew he would never return to us, not completely. This day was one of those rites of passage days when boys turned into men.

He had always been a confidant and independent young man. I'd like to take some credit for that, but I know it's more his nature than my nurture. And like a lot of teenagers, he was so done with high school and ready for college that there was no question he was moving on.

My wife and I moved him into his dorm room and helped him set up his bed, computer, and closet. We'd already spent time on the campus, so he pretty much knew where everything was that was important—food, cash machine, laundry room, and well, that about covers it.

After the couple of hours it took us to get him settled, we lingered. My wife went over last-minute details for the third or fourth time. Be sure to call us regularly. Don't wash the whites and the colors together. Stay on top of your classes.

Then it was time to say goodbye. He was ready; he had things to do. We weren't ready. Especially me. My son was my friend, my buddy, my constant companion. We played catch, shot hoops, watched movies.

I was there at his conception, duh, although I don't remember the exact day that it happened. My wife does, she claims. *It was that Christmas that we were visiting your grandmother in your hometown in that bedroom with the twin beds.* I helped deliver him, which is to say I was the first one to hold him as he burst into the world. I consider that helping, although my wife may disagree.

When he was a baby, I bathed him, fed him, and changed his diapers. As he grew into a toddler, I wrestled with him, pushed him on the swings, and taught him how to go down the big slide. As a kid, he let me show him how to kick a soccer ball, shoot a basketball and throw a baseball. At twelve, we had the talk. Birds and bees. Fun stuff. As a teenager, he pulled away, and I chalked it up to independence and a need to learn his own lessons. At sixteen, we orchestrated a manhood ceremony for him when key men in his life emphasized the true traits of being a man.

He had been a daily part of my life for eighteen years. Now I had to say goodbye?

The hugs at the car as we prepared to drive away lasted longer than usual. The "I love yous" came out in a whisper, from throats tight with emotion. My wife and I climbed into the car, looked back one more time with a wave, and tears filled our eyes. He's our first-born; we hadn't done this before, and we didn't know we'd be so emotional.

My son turned from us and walked back into his dorm room as we drove off. Neither one of us said a word for a long time. We were finding it hard to express how we felt. Proud. Fearful. Apprehensive. Lonely. Sad. Very sad.

I can imagine God felt the same way when He sent his son to Earth. Even though He knew what Christ's mission was and that He'd return, triumphant, in just a few short years. Don't you think God had to be at least a little bummed out? Okay, he's God, I know. Bigger than petty human feelings, stronger than sniveling mere mortals.

God knew how we'd treat His son. We would ignore Him, ridicule Him, reject Him, torture Him and kill Him. God knew that going into it—and He still sent Him.

You see, Christ was the crowning moment of God's master plan. Ever since the Garden of Eden and the rotten trick Satan played on Eve, God set in motion a way that His people could have the same relationship with God that they enjoyed in that garden.

God even predicts it in the third chapter of Genesis: "he will crush your head and you will strike his heel." —Gen 3:15b, NIV

I think that means that a messiah will someday crush Satan. The Old Testament is full of references to a coming savior. God knew from the moment Eve plucked the apple that He would need a way for his people to get back to what they had in Eden. Maybe even before the apple plucking, He had the plan. And Jesus was that plan.

I don't know if God changes His plans like I change mine. I have the patience of a hailstorm; I can be pretty quick to change direction. Maybe God set in motion His plan from The Beginning, and it took all those detours through Abraham, the Israelites, Moses, the prophets, Babylon... Well, it was a long journey before Jesus appeared to rescue us all. Maybe that was the plan all along; after all, he's God, right? If my plans don't work out in a day or two, I'm ready to scrap everything and begin to wonder whether I really should have gone to medical school as my parents wanted.

But God's plan worked. Christ came, He taught, He preached, He condemned, He saved, and He brought people back to life. Then He died, rose up from the dead, showed us how we could do that and ascended to Heaven to return to His father. I imagine God was a little choked up when He got to hug His son again.

I suppose the big difference between God's son and mine is that His boy kept in touch almost constantly. Mine still only calls when he needs money, and maybe the odd occasion when he needs advice.

How do you think God feels when all those boys (and girls) that He created turn away from Him, like my son did that day we dropped him off at college? Lonely. Sad. Very sad.

So call your father. Your human father and your heavenly father. Both are waiting and both want to hear from you. Call today. Right now. Go, go. I'm sure they'd love to hear from you.

SCRIPTURE:

"While he was still speaking, a bright cloud enveloped them, and a voice from the cloud said, 'This is my son, whom I love; with him I am well pleased. Listen to him!' "

—Matthew 17:5

PRAYER:

Dear Lord, thank you for being our Father. Thank you for our birth, our conception, our life here on Earth. Thank you for teaching us, instructing us, coaching us, and letting us learn under your guidance. Thank you for being our "daddy" who loves us unconditionally, like daddies do. Help us to reach out to you, to keep in touch every day, every hour, every minute if we need to. Help us to understand the sacrifice your son gave to us. And help us to remember that we are always your children and that we can always return to the father's lap for love and support. Thank you, Jesus. Amen.

Prius Prejudice

I grew up in a small town in Western Pennsylvania. All of the city streets were quaint and narrow, where the country roads were just two lanes, and you only traveled by interstate freeway if the journey was long. I learned to drive in the slow lane, the right lane, and pass other cars in the left lane. Drive right, pass left.

That served me well until I moved away. Oh, I'd been to the big city and experienced traffic, don't get me wrong, but nothing prepared me for my move to Southern California. My first job transported me from Western PA to the heart of gridlock: Los Angeles.

My initial address was in Huntington Beach. For a kid from the gray, gloomy confines of the Midwest—beach, baby, beach. I just didn't realize everyone else wanted to live by the beach, too.

And that meant traffic. One of my first recollections of life on the West Coast involved commuting (a word I would come to loath over the course of my life) from Orange County up the 405 freeway about 20 miles. (Freeways in California are held in such reverence that they are given titles; the 405, the 110, the 605.) That route in the mornings typically took an hour. I remember one day seeing a fellow in the car to my right reading a paperback novel. He had it sitting on his steering wheel; we were going so slow, he only occasionally had to look up.

I stayed in the LA area five years before moving to Northern California. Nicer scenery I figured, and it was easier to get to know people, too. I was quick to find out that traffic still sucked. This was when the term "road rage" entered my lexicon.

I had several jobs in the San Francisco Bay Area and all involved commuting. (It's really hard to avoid in an area that big with that many people.) By the end of my commuting days in the Bay, I was leaving the house early in the morning before the crunch of traffic hit, then going to the gym for a workout after work to avoid the evening slowdown. By the time I got home, my kids were ready for bed. That meant I didn't see my children in the morning and I only saw them for an hour or so at night. Deep down inside me that didn't feel right; that wasn't my idea of being a great dad.

I finally got up the cojones to quit the corporate rat race (race, ha ha!) and I set up a business in our back bedroom. Seeing my children more than one hour a day triumphed over the perks of corporate life, like a bigger paycheck, benefits that included eye care, and the prestige of working for a "big" company.

But of course I still had to deal with traffic, and habits of life in the right hand lane are hard to break. I had a good friend who claimed that she could "direct" traffic, as though she knew what was about to take place. If somebody cut her off, she'd say, "I knew that was going to happen. No big deal." She claimed it kept her sane and made a fun little game out of traffic. I never got the hang of traffic predictions. My response was more typically, "You dirty SOB. If I ever find you…"

I never did anything crazy out there among the steel gladiators. Mostly, I'd cuss in my car. I don't ever remember getting out of my car to approach another driver the way my buddy who was living in Detroit did. He was stopped at a light when a car approached from behind and slightly nudged his bumper. He immediately rushed out of the car and approached the driver-side window. Without lowering the window or even looking at my buddy, the driver simply raised a huge handgun and laid it against the window. As my friend retreated to his car, he waved and apologized for being in front of that gangster's car. I learned a valuable lesson—it's a battlefield out there.

As I progressed along this path of primal screams in the car to express my frustrations, two trends grew exponentially in the Bay Area: Toyota came out with a hybrid model car called the Prius and the Bay Area upped the number of technology workers imported from Asia. (I'll start out poking a little fun at these trends; then you'll see me slide to the dark side. Just a friendly warning…)

The Toyota website calls the Prius, "the hybrid that started it all." I suppose they mean the trend to equip cars with greater gas efficiency, but in my mind, what the Prius started was the trend that it was now okay to drive slowly on the freeways. What a horrible trend. My philosophy? If you're on the freeway, speed it up, so you can spend as little time on the freeways as humanly possible. But I don't think Prius drivers believe that. They pride themselves on being "fuel efficient" and "environmentally conscious" and "preserving the Earth's resources." I picture them ensconced in their little chrome and carbon cocoons, oblivious to the chaos around them, humming kumbaya songs or listening to CDs with sounds of babbling brooks and ocean waves. Come on, people, move it.

There's a guy in one of the local newspapers—the printed kind, remember those?—whose sole job is to write about roads. I'm not kidding. His whole column is written about traffic, construction, trends, dos and don'ts…you get the picture. Mostly he answers questions from drivers. One of the most frequently asked questions goes something like this: "Isn't it my privilege to drive under the speed limit in any lane I want? Why do these nasty people keeping honking at me, like I'm a terrorist?" His answer was a kindhearted, no. Move way over to the right lane, and if you drive too slowly, you are just as much a menace as the guy speeding by you shaking his fist.

See, it's not my fault I get so agitated; it's the fault of all those Earth friendly people that want to drive 45 MPH on the freeways.

The other trend—the influx of high technology workers from Asia into the communities of Northern California—involves forcing those who came for the jobs to drive automobiles to get to their jobs.

I know you've heard the term, DWI. Driving while intoxicated. In the Bay Area there is this nasty, derogatory, slimy, pathetic term—DWA. Driving while Asian. I almost hate to write that; terrible, isn't it? (I warned you this was going to get dark.) And yet…at times, every once in a great while, almost never, but occasionally, once in a lifetime maybe, it fits. Even my nephew who's Asian American uses the term.

My theory is that with the influx of high technology jobs in the Bay Area since the 1970s, many Asians moved there to pursue their own vision of the great American dream. And many probably had never driven cars, especially the repressed wives of these mostly male tech workers. So, they learned to drive on the freeways of the Bay Area.

Remember when you first learned to drive? What happens first? You take it slow. Driving fast is hard to do. Going slowly allows you to correct mistakes or avoid them altogether. That's fine. I understand; I've been there myself. But that's what country roads are for, learning to drive. Even the Bay Area, with all its people, houses and industry, has country roads. I ride my bike on them all the time. But I hardly ever see people learning to drive on them.

The potentially lethal cocktail mix is an Asian woman driving a Prius. When I see her up ahead, my blood immediately starts to boil. This can mean nothing good at all.

I hope you realize by now that I'm exaggerating the situation to make a point. But it may not be the point you're expecting. My tongue has been planted firmly in my cheek. Okay, not firmly, barely. I wrote the above with a sense of humor, but also with a sense of humility and a sense of failure.

It's a prejudice of mine, I know, the way I classify some people, or judge some people, or even make fun of some people. And I know we need to talk about our prejudices—it's the best way we can work our way out of them.

You remember the story in the Bible of the Samaritan woman at the well. Jesus was waiting there and asked her for a drink of water. Her reply is shocking and shows the prejudice of the times: "You are a Jew and I am a Samaritan woman. How can you ask me for a drink? (For Jews do not associate with Samaritans.)" —John 4:9.

Another version says: "do not use dishes Samaritans have used." The two races didn't mix. A male Jew certainly would never speak to a female Samaritan. It reminds me of those photos from the 1950s in the South where water fountains were labeled black and white. Total segregation. But Jesus crossed that divide, that chasm, that prejudice, by talking to the woman.

Sometimes when I drive, I have fun lambasting drivers who make mistakes or drive like they just learned yesterday. What could it hurt, right? I'm alone in my car, they can't hear me, I don't gesture at them (much, anymore) and I don't carry weapons in my vehicle.

Every once in a while, I get humbled in my car. I do something idiotic or I drive like I got my learner's permit that morning. "He who has never sinned, cast the first stone" always comes to mind when I'm humbled.

But sometimes, I feel like a complete failure when I'm behind the wheel. Like I failed my fellow man. My prejudices flare up unexpectedly the way fireworks do on the Fourth of July. DWA? Really? What *am* I? How did I ever think that way? What if that crude, racial thinking invades other thoughts of mine? How will I ever erase that from my DNA? Is it okay just because I was in my car and nobody heard me? I know my wife heard me several times, no doubt. Have I corrupted her? She has more grace than most any woman I know; what have I done to her snow white DNA?

And if those slurs creep into me while driving, what makes me think they don't creep in at other times? I'm ashamed of my prejudice. I'm ashamed that my grandfather and my father used the N word in reference to African Americans in their neighborhood and other labels they tacked onto people behind their backs. I'm ashamed that I haven't done much to stop my bigotry from seeping into my own children. I'm sure they heard my rants, too.

I'm not sure that anyone is keeping track, but I'm positive that when I spew that crud into the universe, it sticks—somewhere, somehow. It just doesn't evaporate. Maybe it multiplies even. How can I live with that?

I know Jesus doesn't keep track of all the times I fail, all the times I fall short…way, way, way short. He forgives me again and again. I hope I don't have to explain to Jesus, after all these years, why I still harbor those horrible feelings for other people—people I don't even know. How could I ever explain that?

Sometimes it's fun to poke fun. Until it becomes, well…anything but fun. Until it becomes hateful, or prejudicial, or racial, or just plain mean. Where do you draw the line? It's not easy to see; it's often not well-defined.

Or maybe I'm just blind, colorblind. Maybe I've been blind my whole life to my prejudices and the scales on my eyes, like the apostle Paul's, are just beginning to fall away. I don't think every one of us has a little mean streak inside. A part of us that is somehow tainted. Being mean to others isn't a part of being human, is it?

I hope it's not too late. Forgive me—everyone. I know that's not enough, but I had to say it. Pray for me—everyone. Pray for all of us.

SCRIPTURE:

"Do not judge, and you will not be judged. Do not condemn, and you will not be condemned. Forgive, and you will be forgiven. Give, and it will be given to you. A good measure, pressed down, shaken together and running over, will be poured into your lap. For with the measure you use, it will be measured to you."

—Luke 6:37-38

"May the words of my mouth and the meditation of my heart be
    pleasing in your sight,
    O Lord, My Rock and my Redeemer."

—Psalm 19:14

PRAYER:

Lord, forgive me, please. I am such a dolt at times. I forget your example and from my lips, spew filth for my fellow man. I'm a sinner in need of a savior, that's the truth. Bind my tongue, Lord. Strap it down tight. Keep my mouth shut. Turn my mind to thoughts of you. Send your spirit to me at times of need. Keep my heart open to all, sympathetic to all, in love for all. Rip away the scales from my eyes. Help me see. I can't make it without you, Lord. Thank you, sweet Jesus. Amen.

Five Minutes of Solitude

I remember my first computer. I bought an Apple Macintosh in 1986. That was a big decision—to go with Apple instead of IBM, as PC compatibles were then known. It was even hard to find a place that sold Apple products back then.

Apple was a fledgling company with cool products that were easy to use, but they were nothing like the products they are today. The Macintosh had a little tiny screen with no color, a slot for those small disks, and a keyboard and a mouse. There wasn't a lot of software available at that time, but I was just using it as a glorified typewriter, a word processor. The only way to back up any info on the computer was using 3.5 inch floppy disks, although by that time, they weren't floppy, they were rigid. I had no Internet connection; AOL came a little later.

I've been with Apple ever since. Except for the one job I had where I was forced to use the company computer system, an archaic PC-based dinosaur. I don't remember how many times I had to ask, "What is a C drive again and where is it?"

I'm not an early adopter when it comes to new products. I don't jump on the newest technology; I let it mellow a bit so they can work the bugs out first. I did receive one of the first model iPads as a gift, and I bought an iPhone in its infancy, but only after a few models had already been out.

Like most people these days, I suppose, I'm tied pretty tightly to my phone. All my contacts are there, a lot of my notes, my music, my emails. It goes with me most everywhere, although I refuse to keep it in my bedroom at night while I'm sleeping. My wife keeps her phone in the bathroom at night, juicing up, plugged in. Her home office sits downstairs, and I guess that's too great a distance to be separated from her phone. Sometimes, I can hear my wife's phone in there by the sink in the middle of the night, signaling her with an incoming text or email or reminder. It always wakes me up, but never wakes her. I think I hate her phone. Or, her phone hates me.

For the longest time, when my wife didn't immediately answer her cell phone, I'd get mad. I'd say, "What do you have one for if you don't answer it?" She'd, of course, say that she was busy at the time. But I was impatient. I wanted an answer right now! That's the good and bad of these phone computers that we have allowed to become attached to us. We're always reachable—and if we don't answer back right away, we can be deemed rude, aloof, or uncaring.

And now, with the computer we wear on our wrists, we traverse further down that dark road. Yes, the computer watch. Dick Tracy's creator must be smiling from the far beyond. Now your computer will not be in your pocket or your purse, it won't be on your desk in the other room, and it won't be humming in the bathroom, getting its recharge overnight. It will be shackled on your wrist. If you get a message, it will let you know immediately. You'll get buzzed—literally.

Okay, stay with me a while on this one. They already implant computer chips in your body for medicinal monitoring and distribution. Maybe your dog has one inside him so if he gets lost, you can find him. Maybe you're an important international business person or diplomat, and you have a chip implanted inside you, in case you get kidnapped. How long will it be until they get the computer so small—remember, it's the size of a watch now— that they can implant it into your forearm? Instead of touch screen, you have touch skin.

Then how do you turn it off? How do you unplug? How can you ever be alone? If there is no more silence—no more solitude—how do you ever hear that still, small voice of God?

Much has been written today about a society that is bombarded with images, messages, advertisements, conversations, debates, voices, songs, arguments, and, yes, even knowledge. These missiles come from every direction, at any time of day or night, and often without warning. It's hard to escape. If we are "tuned in" or "turned on," there is no more silence. No more solitude.

When my daughter attended high school, she would retreat to her room to do homework after dinner. She was on her computer, the music was blasting, she was texting/chatting with friends, checking Facebook, and studying. Usually in that order. At least she graduated with good grades, and she surely must have developed extraordinary powers of concentration.

How will we suffer as a society if we lose the discipline of solitude? Will our ideas be half-baked, not well developed? I *think* in solitude. I *write* in solitude. My ideas get developed at the keyboard mostly. Sometimes I take notes either in a journal (no, it's <u>not</u> a diary!) or on one of those huge post-it notes, the one the size of a large framed picture. My stories start off as ideas, but they only become real, full, clear as I sit and write.

Here's an exercise for you to try. Put down this book and go find silence— solitude—for five minutes. Simple, right? Go ahead, I'll wait. No rush—take longer if you need it.

No, don't keep reading. Go do the exercise!

Okay, welcome back. What did you experience? The instructions were minimal. I didn't request much. You didn't need to go rediscover the voice of God in your life. Just seek silence for five minutes. Did you remember an item that you needed to add to your grocery list? Good. Did you make yourself a deal to write that thank-you note you've been meaning to send? That'll work. Did you think about a friend or a relative you haven't talked to for a while? Nice—give them a call at the end of the chapter.

Did you simply use the time to relax? If you did, you probably needed just that.

Maybe those five minutes were even more meaningful. Did you pray for somebody who needs help in a miraculous way? Or wonder, deeply, about how you might escape a situation you desperately need to eject yourself from? Did you repent? Maybe you built resolve to mend a fence that's been broken way too long—and came up with a plan for resolution, for recommitment, for renewal. Congrats. I can only imagine how many more accomplishments were achieved in those fleeting five minutes.

What if you develop the discipline to expand that timeframe to 30 minutes or an hour? And what if I added the instruction to "seek God" while you're at it?

There are more than a few men and women in the Bible who got similar instructions: go find solitude, seek God, see what He has to say. Take Abraham. Here was God's instruction:

"Leave your country, your people and your father's household and go to the land I will show you." —Genesis 12:1.

Okay, I admit, I may not be ready to hear that particular instruction. And that's probably not what you're going to hear the first time you've been alone with God in a long time. Maybe Abraham had perfected the solitude discipline.

We don't know much about Abram's life before he became Abraham. Maybe he had an "in" with God. Maybe he spent all his time in communion with the spirit. Or maybe he didn't have as many distractions as we do today. He probably looked to the sky to find the sun to figure out what time it was instead of consulting his computer watch. He probably talked in person to his wife and kids instead of texting, Skyping, or talking via FaceTime. When the sun went down, he probably went outside the tent because he needed some alone time and gazed up at the Milky Way.

I know, I know. You're saying it was a simpler time back then. That all the tasks, commitments, and challenges of today are overwhelming and oh, so time consuming. Yep, my point exactly.

We need the silence. We crave the solitude. Yet we are so poorly trained to find it. So here's my next exercise: go find it.

Set a few boundaries. Carve out some time. Schedule it into your calendar. Don't just read the verse and the prayer below, or put the book down and check your email. They'll still be there in an hour, trust me.

You might want to take your journal (or your diary!) with you. I suspect you and God will come up with a lot of good ideas, and you might want to jot them down. Go, go!

SCRIPTURE:

"After this, the word of the Lord came to Abram in a vision:
'Do not be afraid, Abram.
I am your shield, your very great reward.'
But Abram said, 'O Sovereign Lord, what can you give me since I remain childless and the one who will inherit my estate is Eliezer of Damascus?' And Abram said, 'You have given me no children; so a servant in my household will be my heir.'
Then the word of the Lord came to him: 'This man will not be your heir, but a son coming from your own body will be your heir.' He took him outside and said, 'Look up at the heavens and count the stars—if indeed you can count them.' Then he said to him, 'So shall your offspring be.'
Abram believed the Lord, and he credited it to him as righteousness."

—Genesis 15:1-6

PRAYER:

Thank you, Lord, that you're still there, you still care, and you still speak to me. I am so very sorry heavenly Father that I so seldom listen. Please forgive me. Show me the way back to you—to your side, to your word, and to your voice. I long for the silence, I long for the solitude. Help me find them, Lord. Take away the distractions. Give me the time. I miss you, Father. I want to crawl into your lap and relax in your heavenly embrace. My heart is waiting and my ears turn toward you, anticipating the sound of your voice speaking only for me to hear. I wait for you, Lord. I wait for only you. Thank you, sweet Jesus. Amen.

Woodstock
In the Rearview Mirror

It was originally billed as "An Aquarian Exposition: Three Days of Peace and Music." *Rolling Stone* magazine called it one of the "50 Moments that Changed the History of Rock and Roll." In August 1969 in the Catskill Mountains near the town of Bethel, New York, 400,000 people showed up at Max Yasgur's pig farm for what has become known as the greatest rock and roll show ever—Woodstock.

And I missed it by that much.

The list of performers who played Woodstock is, as we said back in those days, mind-blowing. Here are just a few:

- Richie Havens
- Joan Baez
- Santana
- Ravi Shankar
- John Sebastian
- Canned Heat
- The Grateful Dead
- Creedance Clearwater Revival
- Janis Joplin
- Sly and the Family Stone
- The Who
- Jefferson Airplane
- Joe Cocker
- The Band
- Blood, Sweat & Tears
- Crosby, Still, Nash & Young
- Sha Na Na
- Jimi Hendrix

The music started with Richie Havens at 5:07 p.m. Friday night; Joan Baez closed the first night at 2 a.m. At 12:15 p.m. Saturday afternoon, the music cranked up again and played non-stop till 9:40 a.m. on Sunday morning. After a short break, it started again.

When a rainstorm hit on Sunday afternoon, the music stopped for several hours but picked up again in the early evening; the bands played through that third night. Jimi Hendrix was the last performer, and he hit the stage on Monday morning around 9 a.m.

As an eighteen-year-old in 1969, I was into 3 things in life—girls, rock and roll music and...going to college. I had graduated high school in June and was working that summer to earn money for college, which started in early September. That August, my buddy, Dan asked me if I wanted to go to a concert in New York. It was only a couple hundred miles away.

I asked who's playing? And he said yes. (No, no, sorry, that's an old Abbott and Costello gig.) He was packing his old red Ford, throwing a sleeping bag in the back and heading out with a few friends. Did I want to join him? I said...wait for it...no, thanks. No, I didn't want to go to what would become the symbol of peace and love, rock and roll, sex and drugs for a generation.

I had to get ready to go to college. I think that was my excuse. Maybe it was just that I didn't own a sleeping bag. I wasn't much into camping. Listen to me! Can you believe those excuses? (The story goes that Tommy James and the Shondells were asked to play, but it was pitched to him as, *Yeah, listen, there's this pig farmer in upstate New York who wants you to play in his field.* James declined.) I suspect Dan's plea wasn't as bleak as that, and after all, he didn't know what it would become.

Over the years, I have learned to say "yes" a little more in life. Thank goodness! I've learned to have a little more faith in what's possible.

When Dan and his buddies returned, they were gaga. *Man, you should have been there.* From the looks of them and the old Ford, I wasn't so sure at the time. But they had some pretty wild tales to tell, and even with all the traffic, rain, crowds, and the lack of sleep, food and toilets, they were downright giddy. It might have been the aftermath of the drugs talking, but I don't think so.

If I want to know about Woodstock today, I can check it out online. More than I'd ever want to know about it. Unfortunately, my buddy, Dan died of cancer a few years ago. I miss his spirit, but I still have his testimony about Woodstock. And at least I can tell friends today that I talked to several eyewitnesses who actually were there.

I often wonder what would have happened to the world if the resurrection of Jesus happened a few weeks ago instead of a couple thousand years ago. We'd still have eyewitnesses to talk to, to verify that it really, really, *really* did happen. *Yep, I was there. I saw him, saw the nail marks on his hands, and got the original story of the empty tomb.*

And what about the miracles Jesus performed? Driving out demons, healing lepers, allowing the lame to walk, Lazarus! *Yep, saw most of those, too,* eyewitnesses would say. *I was there, in Lazarus' house, and then he came walking out. He'd been dead a few days; man, it reeked in there. Smelled to high heaven!* (Wait, is that what that saying means? Maybe not, but now it has a new meaning to me.)

It would be nice to have a spoken word recorded, like a music album, of eyewitnesses who were there at the resurrection. I can play that Woodstock album and still get goosebumps when Richie Havens sings "Freedom." What if we had a recording of one of the disciples, like Thomas (the doubting one), saying, *Yes, I didn't believe it at first... He came back from the dead. But, then I saw Him and saw the nail marks on His hands and put my finger in the holes and the hole in His side. It was Him, no doubt about it. He wasn't a ghost; He was alive.*

If the resurrection happened two weeks ago, somebody would have recorded it with a cell phone, you can be sure of that. It would have gone viral by now, would have been seen by millions. Maybe it would have even converted millions or tens of millions. Or more.

We don't see many miracles these days, do we? Okay, Sully landing that plane on the Hudson River may have come close. He saved a lot of lives that day. I've talked to pilots and they say what he did was damn near impossible. But it wasn't like he brought people back from the dead. Maybe he got extremely lucky, one-in-a-million. See, there's the problem. We get so cavalier about miracles these days that we attribute them to luck. After all, doctors bring people back from the beyond; that happens frequently. *Clear! Zap! Okay, he's breathing again!* Thank God! Or thank the doctor.

And, rightfully so, we don't believe TV preachers when they heal a limping man or a woman who comes to the pulpit. They've ruined our conception of divine healing.

Maybe healing, in today's sense of the word, isn't so unique. Even I can heal somebody from a headache, if they're willing. A healer friend taught the technique to me: The sufferer describes the headache in a series of shapes, sizes and colors; they concentrate so much on the description that they actually lose the headache. I'm sure it mostly works on typical stress headaches, not on medically classified migraines, so don't email me or write. Some people don't want me to heal them of the headache. They're afraid of the technique, I suppose, as though I'm doing some kind of voodoo magic on them.

Maybe that's it—we don't *want* to believe. If we believe in the resurrection, we have a lot to lose. We lose ourselves. We have to believe that there is a much, much greater power in the world. We are not, I repeat, *not* the center of the universe—not even the center of *our* universe. And what about everything I'd have to give up if I believed? Jesus said you'd need to give up everything to follow Him. *Everything* is more than most of us, me included, are willing to sacrifice.

And all the eyewitnesses of the resurrection are dead. No recordings, no video, no photos. All we really have is the Bible. Even I admit that some of those statements in the Bible are hard to swallow. Creating the Earth in six days. Adam and Eve were the first two humans. Methuselah lived to be nine hundred-sixty-nine years old? Really? Even if they were something like dog years, with every year equaling seven, that's still about one hundred-forty. Hard to believe, huh?

Faith *is* hard. Having faith when everything around us points in the opposite direction is difficult. Believing because the Bible says so. Taking the word of eyewitnesses dead for almost two thousand years. No proof, no recordings, no video, no photos. Just faith.

But even before the Woodstock album and movie, when my buddy, Dan talked about the greatest weekend of his life, I had only one thought: *I should have been there.* I may never experience Woodstock like Dan did—and I may never know what the resurrection looks like until it happens to me—but sometimes, you just have to believe. Sometimes all you have is faith. And that's enough.

SCRIPTURE:

"Then Jesus said, 'Did I not tell you that if you believed, you would see the glory of God?'

"So they took away the stone. Then Jesus looked up and said, 'Father, I thank you that you have heard me. I knew that you always hear me, but I said this for the benefit of the people standing here, that they may believe that you sent me.' When he had said this, Jesus called in a loud voice, 'Lazarus, come out!' The dead man came out, his hands and feet wrapped with strips of linen, and a cloth around his face."

—John 11:40-44

PRAYER:

Heavenly Father, I admit sometimes I lose faith. I lose my faith in you—and all that you promise. I go my own way; I follow the crowd and lose my path. I am so sorry, Lord. Forgive me. Help me to find my faith again, even when all around me says, no, don't bother, it's not real, how could you believe. Because I do believe, Lord, honest I do. Show me how to keep my faith real, alive, inside me. Help me to talk about it to others, to make it real, to live it every day. Help me to see that others don't have to agree and don't have to believe. Show me your life, your promises and your hope for eternity in the Bible as I read your word. Help me to read it every day. Take away my pessimism. Restore my faith. Restore my love. Thank you, sweet Jesus. Amen.

My Homophobia

Igrew up a homophobe. I don't think it had anything to do with any particular influence from my parents or the section of the country where I was raised. Maybe it was just the time, the 1950s and '60s.

As a young boy and teen, I thought nothing about using words like fag and homo and queer. It was part of the language of "put downs"—that one-upsmanship that boys bantered back and forth. You labeled your male buddies with one of those tags in fun, teasing, to get under their skin a bit. It was simply a game of name calling in adolescence.

Every once in a while, when you would run into somebody you actually thought might be homosexual—as if we had any clue what that might possibly mean—you would utter those names behind their backs. Mostly behind their backs. I don't ever remember confronting anyone with slander like that out loud, but I'm sure it happened from somebody in our group. I was a homophobe in a small pack of boys, tossing whispers back and forth. Others were not so polite.

One boy in our school (I mostly remember him from high school) fit the stereotype we had built. He was quiet, shy, effeminate in his mannerisms and speech, and very un-athletic. That was pretty much our system to judge. He also happened to be brilliant, #2 academically, as I recall, in our high school class of almost 400.

That homophobia didn't leave me when I left adolescence. Sure, I eventually stopped calling my buddies and friends names, but adulthood didn't automatically bring wisdom with it.

I still remember the time I was standing in a pizza restaurant waiting for my pie. I was a cute young adult, not really all that manly-looking. Blond hair, blue eyes, dimples, and brightly colored clothes, which were hip at the time, at least I thought so. The guy behind the counter yelled out, "Pizza, for Bruce!" Some young woman standing nearby commented loud enough for most to hear, "Oh, that figures." Bruce, FYI, is often a label used for homosexuals. Her boyfriend immediately apologized to me, but she reacted like, "What? What did I say?"

I'm not sure much has changed over the last forty years in our language, attitudes, or outbursts. Certainly, the closet doors have been opened in America. Gay marriage is the law of the land, the issue of gay rights is debated at the Supreme Court level, celebrities and other public figures publicly speak of their sexual preference, and many television shows feature gay or lesbian characters.

I want my phobia to leave me, but it won't go away easily.

I understand the analogy of how we treat the gay population to the way African Americans were treated in America. Or, *are* treated in America is more accurate. We brought them to this country as slaves, segregated them from society because of their skin color, and continue to treat them like, well, slaves. Or worse. Shame on us, shame on me.

I understand the right—as in privilege, need, freedom, liberty—to express and live the way you are. I respect that.

I know I am not anybody's judge; that I have no right or responsibility to judge how others live. What other people do in the privacy of their home is none of my damn business. I get that.

I realize that people who have been scorned and abused and labeled and name-called and ridiculed and repressed want and need to stand up and demand to be heard. And apologized to.

And yet…

I understand how some people believe that the Bible speaks out against homosexuality. I've read the verses. I've heard the speeches. I've scanned the blogs.

I also respect the thinking that says that if we believe something is wrong, we need to stand up and say so. That if we don't, we lose the freedom to say anything about that wrong in the future. That if we don't uphold the sanctity of the Bible, and God, who will?

I don't think the Bible is outdated, archaic, or irrelevant for today. But I do appreciate those who believe the Bible can be interpreted with the sensitivities of a changed and challenging world.

I appreciate the type of man/god that Jesus modeled. He accepted everyone, no exceptions. He scorned those who thought they were better than others. He reached out to those whom society had neglected. He offered His love and saving grace to the hurting, the abused, and the defamed. He lambasted those who judged people because they were different.

I understand all that. And most of all, I understand that I don't understand everything. If you're waiting for the solution in this essay, I don't think it's gonna happen.

What I don't understand is what happens to the family.

I've written before how I was raised predominately by women—a single mother and two loving grandmothers—with only peripheral male influence.

I cherish the female influence in my upbringing and know that it contributed to a sensitivity and a loving heart in me that some men my age don't possess. Yet, I regret that I struggled to develop a sense of masculinity. It still plagues me today.

I don't buy into the misplaced male-phobia that is typified with the rants like *"men cause all wars."* To me, that is kin to saying all women should know their place, barefoot and pregnant in the kitchen. We are all unique and can't be labeled accurately in such big statements.

I missed having a full-time father. Men need their fathers—as much as they need their mothers. Like women need their mothers as much as they need their fathers. If you are a man or woman reading those last two sentences and you don't believe that, I challenge you to look a little deeper. The black community in America, with 70 percent of children being raised by only a mother, should at least give you pause to know more about the effects of single parenthood, especially in the area of education success.

I'm not saying that two gay men cannot raise a wonderful daughter. I'm not saying that two lesbian women cannot raise a tremendous son. I'm just wondering what will happen in a couple of generations to those daughters and sons. What happens when we *delete* the masculinity or the femininity from the family? What happens even if we only *dilute* it? And won't that little boy raised by two mothers eventually wonder who his biological father is? Won't that little girl raised by two dads wonder about her real mother? Will those questions be easy to explain? And how will those children be affected by those questions?

Oh, boy, even those musings sound prejudicial, don't they?

Maybe I'm looking at this backwards. Maybe homosexual couples bring a nuance to the family that I hadn't considered. I suspect homosexual couples have to work harder to define the masculine and feminine roles within the family. Two women can teach boys to be tender; two men can teach girls to be bold. Even traditional families have experienced a shift in the roles of mothers and fathers. One of my best friends down the block was mostly a house husband while his doctor wife brought home the bacon. His masculinity wasn't questioned, nor her femininity.

Huh? More tender-hearted men. More bold, confidant women.

I believe God creates us all in His image, each unique with special gifts and talents. When He built the mold for you and me and them, He didn't make mistakes. He didn't get the internal human circuitry mixed up. He made individuals. Each different, each unique, each special.

My homophobia is ingrained in me. Prejudices die hard. They do not go quietly into that good night. They linger like the smell of a dead skunk on the highway. But my prejudices are *not* part of my DNA. They are a learned behavior, but they're not in the blueprint of my soul.

I can overcome my prejudices. With your help. You can overcome yours with mine. And we can all look to the lumberjack as the shining light in the darkness.

SCRIPTURE:

"Don't pick on people, jump on their failures, criticize their faults—unless, of course, you want the same treatment. That critical spirit has a way of boomeranging. It's easy to see a smudge on your neighbor's face and be oblivious to the ugly sneer on your own. Do you have the nerve to say, 'Let me wash your face for you,' when your own face is distorted by contempt?"

—Matthew 7:1-3, The Message

"These words I speak to you are not incidental additions to your life, homeowner improvements to your standard of living. They are foundational words, words to build a life on. If you work these words into your life, you are like a smart carpenter who built his house on solid rock. Rain poured down, the river flooded, a tornado hit—but nothing moved that house. It was fixed to the rock."

—Matthew 7:24-26, The Message

PRAYER:

Lord, sometimes I can't hear you. Sometimes I don't understand what you want from me. I'm lost, I'm struggling. Help me, Father. I can't make it on my own. I'm not smart enough or strong enough. Sometimes, I feel like the prevailing winds sway me and swirl around me, tossing me from side to side and disrupting my balance. I know you are my rock and my foundation. I know that. I don't ever want to lose that. Help me to love you more. Help me to love others more. Help me to overcome my fears and my prejudices. Help me to stand on solid ground. Thank you, sweet Jesus. Amen.

100 Pounds

My mom lost 100 pounds over the span of less than a year. She displayed wonderful willpower to lose that much weight that quickly—and the war in Vietnam was a big reason why.

Mom was a single mother to two very active young boys. We were always hungry and always fed well at home. We didn't eat much junk food, but the calories of the food we did eat was high enough to sustain our busy lifestyles—baseball, basketball, kickball, bicycling and running around all day in the neighborhood.

Neither my brother nor me ever had a weight problem. Mom did. She didn't have great eating habits—okay, maybe they were pretty bad. She loved sweets and snacks, and she never got any exercise except walking to the television to turn the channel. Once we got a remote control, she got no exercise at all.

Even in the 1950s and 1960s, we knew that excessive weight was a health issue. I don't remember making a big deal out of it. I probably felt a little ashamed that she was so big, but Mom was always so loving, her size didn't really matter much.

I've seen photos of her at a young age, and she always seemed to have a little baby fat in her face. She was round, and the round shape was perfectly fine in the '50s. Check out Marilyn Monroe, heartthrob of America. I know weight gain comes too easy for some folks; I try not to be critical of people who just seem to gain weight by *thinking* about eating. I know it's in their genes.

Sometimes in life, health scares like heart attacks or diabetes shock people into losing excess weight. For Mom, the scare wasn't health-related, it was war-related. When the USA drafted my brother into the Army, something shifted for her. He claims he got his college diploma one day, and his draft notice the next. His draft number was 51. I got lucky; mine was 320-something. When your draft number is that high, you don't commit it to memory. The U.S. Armed Forces seemed to conscript enough of America's fine young men before they got much above the number 200. That was 1970, and chances were sky high if you got drafted, there was only one place they sent you—Vietnam.

The day I drove my brother down to the armory—his first stop in his trek to Southeast Asia—my mom vowed to lose the weight. Maybe she felt that if he could sacrifice that much, so could she. I don't remember her diet plan because I was still in college. When my brother returned less than a year later, she had dropped the weight like a hot, double-stuffed-with-cheese-and-sour-cream potato.

She had completely changed her eating habits and showed amazing discipline to stick with the program. The discipline had to come first. Discipline always comes first, then the habit follows. You've heard the old adage if you want to break a bad habit, start a new, good one. But you have to have the discipline to start the new habit.

It's been that way in my spiritual life. Habit follows discipline. My spiritual life grows and glows in times alone with God. Talking with people I know and trust can help me understand, sometimes; they can "people verify" what I'm feeling or experiencing. But for me to connect with my spirit, I need 3 things: morning, coffee and quiet.

But that's just me. Maybe for you: nature walks or classical music or painting or worship singing, however slightly off key.

I have a special place and time. It's at one end of the couch where the morning light shines through the door behind me. It always includes a large mug—maybe two—of freshly brewed coffee from ground beans. I'm alone, and it's quiet. When I try to tap into the spirit when other sound is around, I stall. I used to be able to write while listening to classical music, but I got into that habit when my kids were small, and I had to write in the living room. Now I listen for other voices, especially God's voice, in the silence.

I don't write this to brag that I'm spiritually enlightened. It took me a long time to learn and practice that discipline.

Besides, my mornings don't always work the way I envision. I don't usually have epiphanies. Sometimes the silence is never broken. Sometimes life is just too distracting. Maybe I'm preparing a talk, and I haven't quite figured out the sequence of what I want to say. It rattles around in my brain, and I voice it out, almost phonetically. *Wait! I was praying here; how did I get into that speech?*

I used to get frustrated that I couldn't stay focused on prayer. Now I let it flow. Who knows? Maybe the spirit is supplying the missing words and phrases.

Sometimes in the mornings, I will just concentrate on listening. Trying to still those other voices in my head can be a chore. I haven't tried chanting, except to simply repeat one word, like "Father." Huh, maybe that *is* chanting.

I gave up on my prayer list recently. It's on sabbatical. I used to have a list, numbered by date, in a notebook. The first date was when I first started praying. When I felt that the prayer had been answered, I filled in the second date. It always gave me a sense of God working in my life, in the lives of people I was praying for. Thank you, Lord, prayers answered. Now my prayer time is not so regimented. Rarely do I refer to lists, but that doesn't mean I won't in the future. Right now I seek to be led, not to lead.

But I get distracted. Do you? Sometimes I come up with an idea, and I just want to get to my computer and write about something that had nothing to do with anything I was trying to think about that particular morning. That feeling can be overpowering for me.

I used to feel guilty that I left my time alone with Him without any revelations or even infinitesimal insight. But really, isn't it simply spending the time alone that matters? I'm pretty sure it matters to God. He's molding me. Let Him mold away. I don't need to get in the way so much or dictate how He should work or determine the result He's producing. Move aside; master at work here.

I like the way Marsha Sinetar puts it in her book, *Sometimes, Enough is Enough.* She writes about relinquishing the willful plotting in prayer and in the stillness, letting the Spirit direct our aim.

Sometimes I pick up my Bible and read a psalm or proverb. I still read an old Bible I got when I first found the Spirit. It has a section in front that lists prayers in the book, miracles, or teachings and famous sermons of Christ.

Sometimes I read other authors' insights into the spiritual life. They often illustrate a point in today's language that resonates for me.

Sometimes I just want to be like Mary from the scene in Luke's gospel. Sitting at the feet of Jesus while Martha worked. Open to what He would say. Not distracted by life. Listening in the stillness. Anticipating. Hanging on His every word. Waiting to smile at what He said. How could you *not* smile?

I remember the day my brother returned from Vietnam. Mom was standing in our dining room as my brother walked in the front door. He hadn't seen her in almost a year; he didn't know about the diet. And, goodness sakes alive, he was surprised. She was radiant, beaming, so proud. I think we all cried.

Her discipline had created insurmountable joy in her life and in ours. She had a goal, and she developed the habits to reach it.

Sometimes all you need is discipline. To sit, to read, to listen, to anticipate. To be ready to be radiant, to smile, to beam at what He shows you.

SCRIPTURE:

"As Jesus and his disciples were on their way, he came to a village where a woman named Martha opened her home to him. She had a sister called Mary, who sat at the Lord's feet listening to what he said. But Martha was distracted by all the preparations that had to be made. She came to him and asked, 'Lord, don't you care that my sister has left me to do the work by myself? Tell her to help me!'

'Martha, Martha,' the Lord answered, 'you are worried and upset about many things, but only one thing is needed. Mary has chosen what is better, and it will not be taken away from her.' "

—Luke 10:38-42

PRAYER:

Dear heavenly Father, I long to hear your voice. I'm so sorry that sometimes I get distracted. I let life get in the way of living with you. Help me to settle down, to meditate, to listen. Help me find time to spend with you. Bring me resources, and insights, and authors, and friends so that I may find you more easily every day. Help me to tap into the spirit within me—to let that spirit live and breathe and speak to me. I long to develop the discipline to discover you. Thank you, sweet Jesus. Amen.

Serving from the Left

I grew up in a small town. How small? Well, my two sets of grandparents shared the same driveway. It wasn't that we had a shortage of driveways in the village, just that they lived next door to each other with a driveway in between. If you drove straight through, you hit the Kirkpatrick garage, which Grandmother Kirkpatrick often did, as evidenced by the frequent dents in her Buick. Slant left slightly, and you took the little ramp up to the Arthur garage.

Grandmother Kirkpatrick was one of the best cooks I've ever known. When the family gathered around her dining room table for a holiday meal, you didn't dilly dally in the kitchen trying to chitchat with Grandma. She had work to do, so she told us, "scat, get out, let me do my work." When dinner was finally served, she'd amble into the dining room, perspiration trickling down her brow with a tired but fully satisfied look on her face. Her smile would only broaden when everyone tasted the sumptuous feast.

On the other hand, I'm not sure Grandmother Arthur could boil water. I didn't see her in the kitchen much, except to supervise the cook. You see, the Arthurs employed servants.

You're probably thinking how rich they must have been, and no doubt about it, they were very well off. They lived in a huge house that had a "third floor"—an attic really—that was the servants' quarters, which included two bedrooms, a living room and a bathroom. But the Arthurs had a unique view of servanthood.

They enjoyed traveling to Europe to explore the continent. In those days people took an ocean liner, the cruise ship of the day. I still have a pair of cufflinks of my grandfather's that bear the triple crown logo of the liner, MS Gripsholm, a Swedish vessel they sailed on. My grandparents' trips to Europe were undertaken as much to find a couple that they could sponsor to come to America, as it was for the pleasure of travel. Sponsorship meant that my grandparents would pay for a husband and wife to come to the U.S. to live and work. The couple agreed to work for my grandparents for a specified time, at least until they gained their U.S. citizenship. It was a win-

win situation. My grandparents got servants, probably at a decent wage, and the couple got jobs, room and board, and a chance to better their lives in the good old U.S. of A. And barely ten years after the close of World War II, that likely seemed like a pretty sweet deal to them.

The wife usually performed the jobs of the cook and housecleaner. I don't know if being a good cook was part of the bargain—the food was almost always good, but I certainly tried some unusual meals. No hot dogs and beans were served at that table, but what in the world is tomato aspic, a salad we were frequently tortured with? Google says it's a chilled, jellied salad popular on hot days in 1960s Mississippi. *Huh?* We didn't live in Mississippi, and as far as the grandkids were concerned, these salads were definitely not popular. Let's just say that as a youngster, I got to sample foods of the world. I'll leave it at that.

Typically, the husband's job was as butler, driver, and gardener. Granted, these were not career building jobs, even in the '50s. But as I recall, the husband of the pair was the first to leave my grandparents' employ and strike out on his own in the community. Our town had a number of small factories back then (remember when the U.S. had small factories?) and people could find good jobs in them.

Typically, being a servant isn't such a great gig. Servants hover on the lowest rungs on the social latter and serve rich folks for a pittance. But servanthood at the Arthur residence offered more. Because they served, these individuals had a chance to succeed in life, to be more than they had been, to eventually gain more than they had. To build a better, fuller life.

I never saw my grandparents talk down to the servants. That wasn't their style or their purpose. Sometimes my grandmother would have to correct one of the servants about the proper way to do a particular task. I recall the phrase, "always serve from the left." (She also taught me that serving on the left was most convenient for guests, since the majority were right handed and could easily reach across their body with their right hand.) I believe part of my grandparents' purpose was to teach their employees how to serve and take direction. I now realize that we all need to learn both of those things in life: how to serve others, and how to take direction and learn from it.

Today, servanthood is not highly regarded. I can put this in context. For example, I read a lot about leadership and have at least seven books on my shelf right now that talk about how to be a better leader. However, I don't have any books explaining how to be a better servant. I suppose that's because it's not a career goal for most people. These days, most servants are likely looking for the next job, one closer to their chosen field. Being a servant isn't a career goal in itself. It's like the old days in England when young boys wanted to become a knight. They started as a page, then moved on to squire, and eventually became a knight. Working at servant level today is simply a stop to someplace else. At least that's the goal or the plan.

Jesus is often overlooked as a model of a servant. Sure, we believe He came to serve us in so many ways—He washed feet, He served meals, He bowed down in prayer to His master. But Jesus was powerful, strong and demanding; these are not really the traits of servants as we think of them today. He transformed His day, taught us a new way, and became a king.

We have relatively few servant models today, although Mother Teresa and Princess Diana, and more recently Princess Kate, come to mind. I'm sure there must be others, but I can't think of any.

However, we do have leaders that often adopt a servant mentality. Dr. Greg Boyle is a great example. He's a Jesuit priest in Los Angeles who transforms inner city youth in the barrio by setting up businesses, under the umbrella of Homeboy Industries. Check out his book, *Tattoos on the Heart.* I suspect he would call himself a servant, but I'm sure society would label him a leader in his community. Richard Sterns is president of World Vision US and his book, *The Hole in Our Gospel*, tells the story of his transformation from a highly paid executive living the good life to serving God. But again, he's a leader first; maybe a servant-leader is a good moniker.

So what's so great about being a servant? Why did Jesus wash His disciples' feet as an example of servanthood? Go reread John 13:1-17. When Peter rebelled against Jesus washing His feet, Christ said: "Unless I wash you, you have no part of me."

In essence, he was saying that until you learn to be a servant, you can never know the full extent of why He came. Or…until you serve, you can never really become like Him. Isn't that our goal in life? To become like Christ? Ain't going to happen, Jesus was explaining to Peter, unless you serve.

One time during Easter resurrection week, a church we attended set up "stations" to mimic some of the happenings of the final week of Jesus' life on Earth. One station offered feet washing.

When I knelt in the grass to wash my wife's feet, I felt tears flood my eyes. To be able to humble myself so much in order to serve the woman I love wholeheartedly was a touchstone event in my life.

Try it sometime. Get a pan or bucket of warm water, a washcloth, and a towel. Make it a reverential event. Maybe have some soft music in the background. Maybe pray before you do it, or have a little speech prepared to let your significant other know how you live to serve him or her. It can be life changing.

Want to be a better leader? Go serve the people you lead. Have you ever watched the TV show "Undercover Boss"? Leaders learn a lot about servants, and some will even change the way they lead when they take on the jobs below their position.

Want to be a better father? Serve your children. Get out of the teacher/ coach/ instructor mode and just serve. Better husband? Serve your wife. Get out of the role of criticizer and problem solver and just serve. I always wash the dinner dishes when my wife and I eat at home. It's one small way I find to serve her. You can find others that match your relationship. Back massages, paying the bills, cleaning toilets, doing chores for your spouse that they normally do.

If you've never served meals at a homeless shelter, go do it. It's another life changer. I know a ministry in the San Francisco Bay Area that serves the homeless with a mobile unit that provides the ways and means so the homeless can get their hair shampooed and their feet washed. They get a pedicure, new socks and shoes, and a sense of being served, even for just a few moments. I suspect the servants that do the washing receive much more in return.

Being a servant isn't easy and there aren't a lot of books about the subject, although consulting the Bible is a good start. Don't be concerned if you don't get it right the first time; it's the practice that's important anyway. You'll discover a few rules (serve from the left if it's a meal) but it's really your heart that will lead you.

SCRIPTURE:

"Now that I, your Lord and Teacher, have washed your feet, you should also wash one another's feet. I have set you an example that you should do as I have done for you. I tell you the truth, no servant is greater than his master, nor is a messenger greater than the one who sent him. Now that you know these things, you will be blessed if you do them."

—John 13:14-17

PRAYER:

Humble me, Lord. Show me how to get down on my knees. Help me to let go my pride, my sense of righteousness, my stature, my privilege and my station in life. I want to learn to bow down and serve others, your children. I know it will bring me closer to you and what you stand for. But, I really don't know how to do it, Jesus. Teach me, coach me, show me. I am your servant. I want to serve you by serving others. Present those opportunities and lead me in the way you want me to go. Thank you, sweet Jesus. Amen.

The Bridge

I noticed the sign as I came upon the bridge. *Bridge freezes before road surface.* Before I could figure out what that meant, I found out. I careened down the freeway backwards, completely out of my control. Holy moly!

I grew up in the car business. My family owned a Buick dealership for seventy-five years, beginning in the 1920s and ending at the turn of the 21st century, when our third generation—my brother—finally sold it.

My wife is amazed that I can name the make of most any car from the '50s or '60s and guess within a year or two what model year it was made. (I never mention that there was way fewer cars manufactured back then!) I remember how excited I would get on that special day in September when all the dealers in town introduced their new models. For weeks before, those cars were draped with white sheets, hiding in showrooms across town, ready for the grand revealing.

My dad always had a new car; he never drove the same one for more than a few months. As soon as his cars got close to 1500 miles on them, he sold them, usually to folks he knew in town. They liked getting the newest models with so few miles on the vehicle, and for a nice discount, I'm sure.

One of the first recollections I have as a young child with my dad—actually it's burned into my memory like a rite of passage—involved a trip down one of our town's back roads at night after dinner. There was no traffic on the two-lane road that connected the city limits with a small, private country club on the outskirts of town. I don't remember the specific car, but it was probably red and black; most of his cars were. My dad had probably been drinking; it was his Achilles' heel, a habit he could never break.

Six or seven years old, as I remember, I sat in the middle front seat next to my dad. Once he got the car humming along a pretty straight shot on that stretch of asphalt, he opened up his right arm and pulled me into his lap. We didn't use seatbelts back then, if the car even had them, so it was a smooth and easy transition. I shifted from passenger to co-pilot in one excited-little-boy leap. He put my hands on the steering wheel and slowly withdrew his, keeping them extended in the air, hovering over mine a foot or two away. He looked like a long distance runner crossing the finish line, hands extended up in victory.

Then he punched it!

Man, we were flying 100 miles an hour. At least that's the way I choose to remember it; we were probably going half that speed. But knowing my dad, maybe, just maybe…well, let's just say he liked to drive fast.

I inherited that need for speed. And it very nearly killed me one cold night on the bridge.

Fast forward fifteen years. I'm in college now, coming home for Thanksgiving break. My school was about a five-hour drive from my hometown in northwestern Pennsylvania. I had stayed late that Wednesday before the holiday, probably to turn in a paper or take an exam. I went to school in southern Ohio, and although the weather got cold and gray, it didn't snow much on campus.

My late night trip took me north and then east across Ohio. When I hit the Pennsylvania border I connected with Interstate 79 and headed due north. Scattered precipitation spritzed that cold November evening, but it hadn't snowed yet that winter. That's when I saw the sign I'd seen so often posted along many highways and interstate freeways in the East: *Bridge freezes before road surface.*

As a teenager I thought, okay, good to know, thanks for sharing. What I didn't know—I had to learn that lesson the hard way.

In my four years of driving that stretch of road, many times when it was raining and I passed the exit for Mercer, the rain turned to snow. They call it the lake effect. For 40 or so miles surrounding Lake Erie, snow falls; beyond that demarcation, the snowfall tapers off. Freak of nature.

I cranked it fast up I-79, just south of the Mercer exit. The speed limit was 65 in those days, so I was probably pushing 75, maybe a tick faster. No snow yet. But that sign, that darn sign…

I was coming up a rise and saw the bridge arching over a road below. As soon as I hit the overpass, my world turned 180 degrees as my late model Buick spun out. I found myself traveling down the freeway backwards at 75 MPH!

I can recall that, in my panic and fear, several faces flashed in front of me. I no longer remember who they were, and they weren't characters in stories. Just faces, people I knew. People I suppose I wanted to remember in case it was the last time I would see them.

I didn't have a lot of options in that predicament. I kept my hands on the wheel and steered; what else could I do? Even today, looking back, I'm at a loss as to how I survived it. Hope, pray, duck?

Luckily, the highway was empty. No cars ahead of me, no cars behind. My Buick gradually slowed down, veering to what was now on my left side, toward the shoulder. The car came to rest, shuddering and bumping along as I gradually applied the brake, with a slight thud on the guardrail. The engine conked off. I suppose it wasn't used to running so long and hard in reverse.

My heart in my throat—that's no exaggeration—I shook from fright. I took a minute or three to calm down, but the nose of the car slanted toward the highway in the wrong direction, so I knew I had to get moving. I so wanted to get out of the Buick to check for damages, but I didn't know if I could even stand, I was so rattled.

I restarted the engine, did a U-ey across the highway, and headed north again toward home. I know I never went faster than 35 MPH the rest of the way.

When I arrived in my hometown, I pulled off on a side street to assess the damages. I rubbed my bare hands along the side of the car that had been pinned to the guardrail, wiping away the grime of the highway but seeing no slashes or gouges. Just one small dent in the bumper. I was a happy boy; shouts of joy pierced the cold night air.

At the time, I chalked it up to luck. Divine intervention never entered my thinking. But now, I'm not so sure. I didn't have much of a relationship with God at the time. Jesus was simply a guy in Sunday school. I hadn't been to church since I left for the university.

But does that mean God wasn't watching over me? Does that mean God wasn't in charge of my life on that particular evening in November?

For those of you who accepted Christ at an early age, you have an advantage. You can look back on your life and see the hand of God on your shoulder, on your footsteps, on your life. Or on your car.

For those of us who come to the Lord later in life—I was forty—it's easy to look only at our life since we came to Him. We tend to put away those chapters before knowing God, writing them off as childish, immature, or well, just plain stupid. Born again means a do-over, a mulligan, a restart. Let's not relive the past; let's write a new future.

But we were chosen way before we accepted His invitation. We are not like foster children, born of another family and then suddenly, after a trial period, invited to join a new one. We are all children of God, made by His hands in His image. Some of us forget that or never acknowledge that in the first place, but it doesn't make it less so.

Some of us get trapped into believing that He is an angry or vengeful God, full of rules and regulations, and if we stray off course—oh my goodness, if we sin—He gets mad at us, closes the door to His throne room, and disappears from our life.

Nope, He's not like that at all. Read a little Joyce Meyer, especially her book *God is Not Mad at You*, if you think that way.

As I look back at my life, I see His hands on my shoulder. Sure I did stupid things, but nothing too awful. I tried marijuana, often, and I inhaled. I ingested my share of beer and still do. I indulged in premarital sex as often as I could. I was bad, mean, reckless, daring, inconsiderate, uncaring, and wild at times. But, I was always a child of God. And He never lost his connection with me. He sometimes punished me, deservedly so, but He never banished me. He never let go. He will *never* let go, even if I lose touch with Him.

I can now see that trip of terror backwards down the freeway in a new light. I imagine God, busy as He was that evening, suddenly getting a glimpse of the Buick doing its about-face and somehow guiding me to the guardrail. Was it a super breath, like Superman, putting me back on course? A touch of his heavenly hand, steering the car in the only path that leads to safety? A light touch on the steering wheel? Beats me. Don't really care.

I'm just glad He *was* there. I'm glad He always will be.

SCRIPTURE:

"He replied, 'You of little faith, why are you so afraid?' Then he got up and rebuked the winds and the waves, and it was completely calm."

—Matthew 8:26

PRAYER:

Thank you, Lord, that you never forsake us—that you never leave us or abandon us. Thank you for caring for every moment of our life. Thank you for your Spirit that steers and guides us. Thank you for your Word that instructs us and teaches us and tells us of your amazing power, grace and mercy. Help us to remember how much you love us, cherish us, and protect us. Help us to remember you are a loving father, our daddy, who grabs our hand in times of peril, who reaches out for our grasp when we need a loving touch, who is always within sight and sound of our cry for help. I pray sweet heavenly Father that I will always remember how much you love and care for me. Thank you, sweet Jesus. Amen!

Eagles

As a child of the 1950s, the first record album I bought for myself was *Elvis Presley's Greatest Hits*. I may even still have it in my collection. That stack of wax has survived numerous cross-country moves and the influx of new technologies. Remember 8-track tapes? Elvis and his hits are now buried deep in a storage facility in Southern California. But it will live another day! There are just some days you want to listen to Graham Parker and the Rumor or…don't hate on me…The Knack!

I also remember the first concert I attended. Sometime around 1967, I double-dated to see The Fifth Dimension, who were on a roll at the time: it was the Age of Aquarius and we had to let the sun shine in. My wife and I still attend a few concerts each year, although it's hard to find music we both like. I crave rock and country; she enjoys R&B and jazz. Whichever group we see, one of us has to compromise a bit. She once went with me to see Jackson Browne, but once was enough. One Valentine's Day, I bought her tickets to see Al Jarreau, and I had fun, but not too much.

The very best concert I ever saw happened on New Year's Eve, 1974. I had just moved to Los Angeles and was into the live music scene. In LA in the 70s you had many choices of venues, including small clubs in Hollywood (where I saw the Tubes), auditoriums like the Shrine (the first time I saw Jackson) and stadiums where the Dodgers and Angels played. I splurged for those New Year's Eve tickets, fetching first row balcony seats from a ticket store (yes, they existed) to see the hottest country rock group in the nation, the Eagles. (Actually their real name I've found out over the years is simply Eagles, but if you don't put the "the" in there, it sounds like your conserving words for no apparent reason. Don't believe me? Check out any album. There is no "the" there.)

The concert started later than usual, around 9:00 p.m., with an opening act nobody had heard before, Dan Fogelberg. He went on to be huge in the 70s and 80s. A brilliant guitarist by the name of Joe Walsh, who had limited fame with The James Gang, played alongside. Of course, Walsh joined Eagles (see, it barely works) soon after and is still in the band. The Eagles (oh, better) followed and after a lively set, left the stage for a short break around 11:30. They returned and rocked well into the LA New Year night. As encore after encore ensued, other musicians from the LA scene joined in, including Linda Ronstadt, Jackson Browne, Walsh, Fogelberg, and J D Souther. That was 40 years ago and I still remember it well.

So when the Eagles did their latest farewell tour—they've done half a dozen, at least—with a stop near our hometown, I got tickets. My wife, trouper that she is, said she'd enjoy it, and I knew she would—but probably not too much.

The concert started at a reasonable time on a weekday, 7:30 p.m., so the group of us decided to leave work early to beat traffic and have dinner near the show, which was about 40 miles away. Usually when my wife and I are going to an event, as we get in the car, one of us asks the other, "Got the tickets? Your wallet? A little cash?" This time that didn't happen. Probably should've. Uh, oh.

Halfway to the venue, my wife asked, "Got the tickets?"

I immediately swerved two lanes to the exit and gunned the car through the off ramp. Almost killed us both. You can guess the answer to her question. Now I had to maneuver my way back home—the tickets were sitting on my desk—and then fight traffic on the return trip. We were definitely going to miss dinner. My mind started to go directly south. *We'd probably get stuck in traffic, miss the concert entirely. I'm an idiot, incompetent in all things.* I am really getting mad at myself and everyone all around me.

The truth of the matter was, none of that was going to happen. Yes, traffic could be a problem and I'd had lunch so missing dinner wasn't going to kill me. Heck, my wife is lactose intolerant and eats only gluten-free food, so she probably wasn't going to find much on the menu she could have anyway.

But my rational mind had gone bye-bye. All I could see were cars, cars and more cars, no place to park when we got there 'cause everybody else had arrived early or on time. No dinner, big crowds, laughing friends. Now I'm really getting upset, trying to set land speed records, winding through traffic. I was beyond consolation; believe me, my wife tried.

I can look back now and see the folly of my thinking. At the time, I was fogged in by constrictions of time and malcontent. We were going to be late and it was solely my fault. (Aren't you and I both glad I didn't say to my wife, "Well, you didn't ask me if I had the tickets!") In hindsight, I didn't have too much to be concerned about. My wife offered to drive, which would have taken me away from the combat arena of traffic. We had reserved seats. I knew the city like the back of my hand and every parking lot within blocks of the concert. I was also driving a beautiful car, sitting beside my beautiful wife of thirty years of a happy marriage. Okay, not so happy that night, but in general, wonderful. We were heading to a concert of one of my all-time favorite bands with friends I always enjoyed.

Sometimes, I lose my fragile hold on being content for inconsequential reasons. I lose track of the big picture. I forget to ask myself: What's the worst that can happen? (You mean it can get worse than this? What are you thinking, that I could crash the car?) No, no, really; it can always be worse.

If we truly believe that God is good, that He never gives us more than we can handle, and that we have a reserved seat in the greatest venue in the history of eternity, how can we let little everyday hiccups disturb us? Am I the only one who goes a little crazy when life takes a detour?

I look back at that Eagles incident with regret and shame. Why am I having such a problem grasping contentment? Don't get being content confused with satisfied. I really don't ever want to be fully satisfied. I don't mean satisfied, as in how we feel after a nice dinner. I believe that there are too many wrongs in the world to be satisfied. I may be satisfied after that dinner, but unsatisfied that so many in the world go to bed hungry.

Contentment is different, distinct. In his book *Awakening the Quieter Virtues*, Gregory Spencer writes that detaching yourself from total satisfaction is a key to being content. You have to be satisfied with being unsatisfied, but don't read that to mean dissatisfied. It's about being strong in your hope, strong in your belief and strong in your faith. Spencer lists a few keys questions to keep your contentment needle right where it should be:

- "Who am I? A child of God, rescued by Jesus, alive with the spirit."
  —I John 3:1; 1 Peter 3:18; and Romans 5:5

- "What is important in life? Loving God and my neighbor."
  —Mark 12:28-31

- "What can separate me from what is important? Nothing."
  —Romans 8

- "What can I do to make things better? Work and give thanks."
  —Colossians 3:17

- "What can I do about the things I can't control? Put hope in God."
  —Psalm 42:5

In my journal, I have written about Spencer's way of centering himself when circumstances seem ready to overwhelm. *This is the life I've chosen,* he chants. When nothing seems to help, Spencer at least wants to be able to say: *This is the situation where God is instructing me.* Those mantras will help.

I can see that those questions would help focus me back to being content. Luckily, I don't go off the deep end too often.

And yes, we missed dinner but had time enough to grab a beer before the concert. Eagles...no way...The Eagles will probably do another final farewell tour soon so I have another chance to enjoy them. My wife probably won't go with me...for obvious reasons.

SCRIPTURE:

"Meanwhile, live in such a way that you are a credit to the Message of Christ. Let nothing in your conduct hang on whether I come or not. Your conduct must be the same whether I show up to see things for myself or hear of it from a distance."

—Philippians 1:19, The Message

PRAYER:

Lord, help me focus on YOU. Help me to realize how much I have, how little I need and how blessed I am. I pray that I have a spirit of giving thanks to you for the blessings you've bestowed on me. Help me to learn not to let little things distract me from the big things you and I are working on in this life. Help me to recognize early on those situations that can steal my contentment. Help me to tap into your spirit, Lord, to settle and calm me. Help me to be content in all that you are, all that you promise, and all that you deliver. Thank you, sweet Jesus. Amen.

The Pessimist

Two five-minute phone calls in October of 2008 almost put me out of business. Both came from clients—my two best clients—canceling their marketing contracts with me. By the time 2009 emerged and the Great Recession had its claws in the economy, my business was off 75 percent. Dropped like a rock.

Over the span of the next several months, I cringed every time I looked at our savings statements. As springtime began to blossom early that year in California, our savings, much of it invested in the stock market, had plummeted 50 percent—and it was still heading south like a bullet. The bloom of spring turned to doom in my mind.

I remember experiencing the same feelings as I watched the Twin Towers fall on 9/11. Fear. Anxiety. Impending blackness. Dread. Doom.

My mind immediately began to envision the "worst that could happen." It wasn't the "worst that can happen" planning technique in which you put all the bad things in the negative column (the worst) and all the good things in the positive column. *Oh, that's the worst that could happen? That's not too bad.*

No, that's not the way I thought. The worst that I imagined was borderline catastrophic.

I saw us losing our home, our business, our savings. And I clearly saw myself waiting tables to make a living. I didn't panic or throw myself out the window, but I did lose sleep and weight from worry.

Here's what I learned from that experience: two kinds of people live in the world—optimists and pessimists. Most are born one way or the other. I don't know many optimists that have turned into pessimists, but I hope like heck that some pessimists can acquire the skills to become more optimistic. Here's why.

I'm a pessimist. I've tried to learn to be otherwise, but with little success. My wife Nancy is an optimist. I attempt to explain to her that we balance each other out—my pessimism, her optimism. But optimists don't look at it that way. My wife will say: "Why not look on the bright side? It's always more uplifting!" And I'll counter with: "Yeah, but what's the worst that could happen? We have to plan for that, don't we?"

I'm sure I frustrate her to no end.

Recently, I looked back at my personal journal to see how I handled the funk that shrouded me in early 2009. I'd been mired in pessimistic goo lately, brought about by much uncertainty in my life, so I needed to revisit past successes.

My first idea was to get back into saying affirmations. I remembered as a young man using affirmations every day. I searched my computer, but couldn't find my originals. Later that evening, I was able to recall the gist of most of them since I had repeated them almost every day for a decade or more. Back then, I affirmed that I was smart, resourceful, a good provider for my young family, a loving father, and a supportive husband. Also, that I was healthy and did the things I needed to do to stay healthy. I had affirmations for my business, finances, future, and even, get this, for my outlook on life. I suspect I was affirming that I could turn myself into an optimist.

As I look back, that's the way my life turned out, the way I had affirmed it. I've been married thirty-two happy years. Both kids graduated from respected colleges and are on their way to successful lives. I still exercise, maintain my weight, keep my blood pressure and cholesterol down, and have had no health scares. My business ran successfully for over twenty years. I saved, recovered all that we lost during the recession, and am financially secure for the future.

Those journal notes of 2009 also spoke to a need to shift my focus in life, from a state of scarcity to a state of abundance. True, I didn't have the business or savings levels that I had before the recession, but I had some of both to build on. I still had my health, and I still had the love of my life, my wife, by my side. I could find joy in life—if I looked in different places and with a different attitude. I had many things in life I could appreciate— my education, my business skills, my children, our friends, our extended family—the list could go on and on, especially with today's 20/20 hindsight. Today, I can see that learning to appreciate what we *have* instead of what we've lost (or haven't found yet) is a powerful tool, especially for proclaimed pessimists.

Tucked away on page 84 in that 2009 journal was a single bullet point under the title of *Things of Abundance in My Life*: spiritual fulfillment. Just those two words.

Later in the month, I sketched out a daily morning devotional time that made me concentrate on abundance with a spiritual slant. I began to get a picture in my mind of better days. I prayed for more abundance of:

- Peace of mind (free of worry and stress)
- Health (in my case, more exercise, less alcohol)

- Love—for myself and others
- Joy (which I connected closely to a view of heaven)
- Appreciation
- Blessings

I started to reprogram my life GPS. From a global view, I saw that where I was in life was a better place than I thought. And I envisioned the position I wanted to be in the future as a much better place—full of abundance.

Throughout the process, I was humbled by the fact that I could acquiesce in life to my wife, my kids, my job, and my friends when I needed to. But when times got bad, I had a hard time acquiescing to Jesus. Even though my prayers were asking for His abundance in my life, I was trying to do it all on my own. I noticed that when impending financial ruin was upon me—okay, financial setback might be a better evaluation—I reverted to my pessimism instead of to my Lumberjack Jesus.

I asked the question in my June 2009 journal entry: how do I put my love of Jesus above my fear of failure in life, whether financial, business, or... whatever?

My answer? We need to understand the truths of God. For the pessimists in the crowd, let's review a few that apply:

1. "God is good."
   —1 Timothy 4:4

2. "He wants you to be joyful."
   —Psalm 45:7

3. "You have nothing to fear."
   —Psalm 84:11

4. "God brings good, not evil."
   —3 John 1:11

5. "He is the light and your salvation."
   —Psalm 27

6. "His grace is sufficient."
   —2 Corinthians 12:9

7. "Love wins."
   —1 Corinthians 13:4

8. "God wins."
   —Revelations 20

As a pessimist, I can't let the dread win. I have to concentrate daily, heck hourly, on what is good and abundant in my life. God delivers *daily* everything I need to survive—and to thrive. That's what is meant in the Lord's Prayer when Jesus says, "our daily bread." He is everything we need this day and the next. And the next, and the next. Daily, hourly, every minute, and every second.

My new Optimist Creed: better bread than dread.

I'm going to write that one down in my new journal.

SCRIPTURE:

"But he (Jesus) said to me: "My grace is sufficient for you, for my power is made perfect in weakness." Therefore I will boast all the more gladly about my weaknesses, so that Christ's power may rest on me. That is why, for Christ's sake, I delight in weaknesses, in insults, in hardships, in persecution, in difficulties. For when I am weak, then I am strong."

—2 Corinthians 12:9-10

PRAYER:

I lose it sometimes, Lord. I lose focus on you. I lose your love somewhere. I lose my trust in you. I only rely on myself and my ways, however dastardly and deceitful they are. I am so sorry, Lord; please forgive me. Please reassure me. Please repossess me. Deliver me from the brink. Rescue me when I fall. Help me to look for you, to gaze upon you, to delight in your sight. Shine your love, your joy, your light, and your salvation all over me. Blind me, Lord. Blind me to my darkness, so that I might see only you, only your light. Keep me in the comfort of your arms, forever. Thank you, sweet Jesus. Amen.

The Ride

Bicycle riding is one of my great passions in life. I got my first Raleigh bike in high school, dabbled with riding in college and really got into it when I moved to California in the mid-1970s. The Golden State is perfect for bike riding; it's cool in the winter, not too hot in the summer. I'm what they call a "roadie"—I ride on paved roads because I can go fast, long and hard. Now, those are relative terms. Some younger riders may ride 100 miles a day; I'll do around 20, two or three times a week, maybe climbing to 100 miles a week in the summer when the days are long, work is slow and my energy is at a peak.

I ride because it's therapeutic. Sure, it's good for my health, keeps my weight down and heartbeat up, cholesterol under control. But I also need the time alone.

I no longer participate in team sports, all back slapping and high-fiving. I now relish the solitude and challenge of pushing myself to test my self-prescribed limits. But that's just me. I work alone, too, for the most part. I suppose I've always enjoyed the battle of man against mind. I figured out early on that I was always my biggest enemy. My mind said I couldn't accomplish something, but my body is always up for proving the intellectual side of me wrong. And I don't like to depend on other people for my accomplishments. I'm my own boss. Actually, that's probably why I work alone; I'm way too independent to work for someone else.

I can get independent with God at times, too. Much of the time, I submit to His will when I can decipher it, and follow where I believe He is leading me. And I'm happy about it. But then the Adam in me surfaces and I act exactly how I want. I don't ask God to lead. I don't listen when He whispers to me, and I don't even consider His input.

A recent bicycle trip through the windmills and vineyards in Northern California illustrates my point. In the early morning of a summer Saturday I had mapped out a relatively easy 30 mile ride from one of my bicycling books, circa 1985. I stuffed a hand-scribbled map of the route into my jersey back pocket, loaded bike and gear into my car and drove into the wine country. Before I jumped on my bike, I studied the map and calculated the water and food I'd need for the journey. I even knew of a gas station with a convenience store attached in case I needed replenishment.

As I settled into a steady pace, I relied on practiced techniques. I pushed hard, but not beyond my limits. I waited for my heart rate to settle down as I climbed hills, I rode under control as I descended. I checked the map whenever I had a question.

Then an urban sprawl smacked me upside the head. A new housing development had sprouted unexpectedly. The map was useless; me, clueless. We aren't in 1985 anymore, Dorothy. The right-hand turn I was looking for was nowhere to be found. My original route was pretty much a circle. Cyclists like to make lots of right hand turns; that way they don't have to cross traffic turning left. I knew if I just kept peddling, I would eventually hit a familiar road where I could turn right and find the next segment of my trip.

I just didn't know it would be another 7 miles down the road. Seven miles doesn't sound too far. However, if you add up 7 miles down, 7 miles across and 7 miles back, that's 21 miles. I made the extra-long loop, stopped to ask directions (yes, my wife would be proud) and found my way back to a map coordinate I recognized. I'd traveled an extra hour and a half, but I was conserving energy and food so I was in pretty good shape, not too worried. But I should have been.

The detour took me into the mid-90s heat of the afternoon, and as my legs got heavy, my water and food depleted quickly. The pinnacle of the ride was a huge hill at the 25-mile mark. The 25-mile mark of the 30-mile ride. Even though my mind was zapped, I had enough sense to make out that if I added the extra 21 miles to the 30 miler I was planning for...well, you do the math. That's 51 big ones.

At about 40 miles, I got an epiphany. I started praying. Better late than never. God, help me, I prayed. I'm a little out of my element here and I sure could use your help. My legs were dying, my water running low, my food gone. Okay, God, now it's time for you to show up. I'm at my end, will you please take over? I've done all I can do; now I guess I'll submit and ask for your help. Just writing those words, it seems really lame, doesn't it? God shouldn't be my last resort.

So there I was, wasted, out of food and even in my impaired state, I could tell dehydration had set in. I pushed on. I knew if I slowed my pace a bit, I could make it over the hill; then it was a straight shot and mostly downhill to my car. You're with me, aren't you, God? You can buy into that plan, can't you? Just give me a sign, will you?

As I climbed the hill, it looked much bigger than my book had indicated. My mouth was parched, water bottles empty, legs shot and I was gasping for more air. At least I have my prayers, but obviously, God was working on something else. He didn't seem to be hearing me.

With sweat pouring down my face and stinging my eyes, I had placed my sunglasses into the vents of my bike helmet so I could swipe at my eyes with my gloved hand to clear my vision. As I rounded a curve and saw the hill take a dramatic lurch straight up, I gasped. Then I cried out, "Jesus, help me!" It was no idle plea; I was in trouble.

And God responded. At the very instant my cry bolted skyward, my sunglasses popped off my helmet and crashed to the pavement. I don't mean they slipped off. They literally jumped off my helmet. So I did the natural thing—I stopped. Right in the middle of the hill. (I never do that; it's almost sacrilegious in my sport.)

The hill was so steep I knew I'd need a big push to get up enough speed just to start the climb again, so I rested a bit. I found a little shade, cleaned my shades and caught my breath. Then I heard a whisper. It said to me, "You're a tough one, I almost had to knock you off that bike to get you to rest." I'm stubborn, God, what can I say?

It's like that old joke with the religious man caught in a raging flood. He flees to the roof of his house as the waters rise and prays to God to save him. A man in a rowboat paddles by and offers a ride, but the man refuses. "I'm waiting for God to save me," he says. Then a helicopter appears and circles above, offering a ladder to safety, but the man refuses. "I'm waiting for God to save me." Finally the waters rise, the man drowns and he lands in heaven. "God, why didn't you save me," he asks? And God answers, "Well, I sent the rowboat and the helicopter, what else were you expecting?"

God was telling me to stop and rest, and I was pushing on. Beyond my limits, past my reserves. I hadn't been listening. How many times in our life are we literally hell bent on accomplishing our own agendas and ignoring God? Even when we ask for God's help, we ignore Him.

Sometimes the best way to hear God is to stop and listen. And often the stopping is the hard part. We can claim to listen all the time to God, but unless we clear the lines of communication, the signal can get blocked. I can't rub my stomach and pat my head at the same time, maybe I can't be doing something and listening at the same time. Maybe I just have to stop and listen, not just slow down a little. Get off the bike, find some shade, and listen. Then listen some more.

SCRIPTURE:

"I am the vine; you are the branches. If a man remains in me and I in him, he will bear much fruit; apart from me you can do nothing. If anyone does not remain in me, he is like a branch that is thrown away and withers; such branches are picked up, thrown into the fire and burned. If you remain in me and my words remain in you, ask whatever you wish, and it will be given you."

—John 15:5-7

PRAYER:

Heavenly Father, show me how to listen to you. I cannot live my life without your voice, Lord. Help me to build that communication bridge so that I do less talking and praying, and more listening. Help me make time and put away distractions to really listen to you. Help me prioritize my day, each day, so I spend extended time with you. Help me to clear my mind of interfering chatter, to-do lists, and agendas. Help me settle my soul so that I'm open to your voice. Holy Spirit, come alive in me to guide me to his voice, his call, his touch, his love. Thank you, sweet Jesus. Amen.

Wyoming

It's midmorning in Wyoming's Bighorn Mountains and buried deep in the canyon's hole, we haven't seen the sun yet. But we anticipate it will hit our backs about the time we emerge at the top of the climb. And that's the sight we're almost giddy to see, our final destination for the morning's ride—Red Canyon.

The horse seems to know the way without any help from me. He's probably been this route a thousand times before, and he's simply working by rote instead of by the reins. The ground is slick and mucky from the rain the night before and the trail is littered with rocks. But his steps are sure, practiced, and even when one hoof slips, the other three find solid ground.

We are winding our way through a creek bed, following a trail at the base of an uphill climb that's soon to follow. Crisscrossing the creek three or four times already in the first hour of the ride, it's hard to imagine this small tributary of Wolf Creek, barely 2 feet wide, has helped carve this canyon.

Eight of us, fraternity brothers and graduates of the same Midwestern university, gather at a small dude ranch in north central Wyoming every third year or so. We've made it a ritual to keep our relationships alive and have rendezvoused religiously over the past forty years in locations all over the country. Our latest favorite is this ranch, and while I call it a dude ranch, it might not fit the description you have in your mind. There's a swimming pool, but in the half dozen times we've been here, I've never seen anyone in it. There's a hot tub and a couple of the guys bring swimming suits and soothe tired bones. But, this is not a spa with horses. This is one of the oldest dude ranches in the West; it celebrated its one-hundred and twenty-fifth anniversary a few years back. Not much fishing, not much hunting; just riding. That's the way we like it.

I first visited the ranch as a teenager. My family had been coming since the 1930s, back when my grandparents were young. A couple of years after my grandfather died, my grandmother wanted me to experience the ranch. She'd taught me how to ride and I'd seen the pictures of the ranch and heard her best stories. My grandparents had instilled in me their love of the West, and yet, I'd never been there. Our visit turned out to be one last ride for my grandmother and the first of many for me.

When I had my first midsummer adventure on the ranch, I was still in high school and most of the summer help were college girls, who waited tables or cleaned cabins. Once their morning chores were done, we'd saddle up and head out. Same thing in the afternoon, if they could get away. The evenings were filled with campfires, Coors, and cuddling—I was playing with the big girls now. I even learned how to square dance, although it felt more like a combination of arm wrestling and touch football to me.

Thirty-five years later, I learned one of the eight fraternity brothers had visited the ranch, too, and recommended it as a great place for the next rendezvous. Serendipity for sure, and I was ecstatic to return. Now, as an adult, every time I revisit the ranch, I slip into my old riding blue jeans, tug up my boot socks, and stomp my cowboy boots on tight. I feel right at home.

As we wind our way to Red Canyon, I'm comfortable on the horse. By the end of the summer, he's tired and worn from double day rides beginning in May. Intractable burrs nestle in his mane and tail; he'll have to wait for fall for a good grooming. As I gaze at his withers and shoulders, I see nicks and cuts, healed over from many summers of traversing the mountains, getting gouged by rocks and trees. These are not show ponies, but rugged western mounts ridden hard all summer long. I lean right to look at his forearms (his upper leg to you and me). They're well-muscled and lead down to his knee, cannon (lower leg) and hoof. All chiseled by years of work and years on the mountains. His hoofs cla-clump in rhythm and I concentrate my body to connect and stay in his stride.

Now his job is working up the mountain. He pants and he sweats, even in the cool morning air. He plods; he's in no hurry and I'm content to let him make his own pace. If he stops for a breather, I take the time to take in the scenery.

The Bighorns cut through Northern Wyoming into Montana, a crescent-shaped range traversing some 200 miles in a northwest direction. A spur of the Rockies, the Bighorns are separated from the rest of their parent range by the Bighorn basin. The highest peaks in the range climb to almost 13,000 feet. The ranch we visit sits in the basin at about 4500 feet right at the feet of the Bighorns.

The Roosevelt Trail, named after Teddy, who frequented the ranch on his many trips West to find health and bravado, is one of our favorites and an offshoot of this Red Canyon route. But it's treacherous at points.

Having ridden it many times, I know the horses hug the mountain rim trail, scattered with shale. We hang on to saddle horns and try to look down. Sometimes we just hang on and scrunch down, leaning forward as the horse climbs and trusting that he'll find his way and his footing. The horse always does and our job becomes not falling off, even when the mount leads us through trees and scrubs, with branches sticking out trying to poke or prod us off. At the top of Roosevelt, you can see Montana, 50 miles away.

That was yesterday's ride; today's isn't as dangerous or as long. Red Canyon splits to North Red and South Red, with the ranch sitting in between. Wolf Creek slides effortlessly down from the peaks, past the ranch and onto the plain. It looks like the canyons have been heaved up from beneath by a behemoth.

As we crest and emerge from the trees, South Red comes into view. The canyon is definitely well-named. It's red, although maybe it's better described as burnt orange or terra cotta, similar to the red dirt in Hawaii or Georgia. From afar, the canyon looks like an ocean wave, flowing up from the left, cresting, and then falling again as your eye scans right. Spruce trees line the bottom and a few have crept up the sides, hanging on. Layered ridges of red rock stack a thousand feet high. More trees top the ridge, but are scattered sporadically, every hundred feet or so. The morning's ride will take us around the rim, to the top, and back down the other side to the ranch. It's not Roosevelt, but it is spectacular. We never tire of the view and do this same ride every trip.

We are an interesting group, exactly the same age and with similar backgrounds. Entering the small, private liberal arts college in 1969 and spending four years together, we've scattered across the U.S., from California to North Carolina, and parts in between. I've never had closer friends and know I never will. If we haven't seen each other for four or five years, we pick up the same conversations as if we left them the day before, never missing a beat, or a putdown, or a joke.

It's always September when we're there, and the ranch has weathered the summer rush and is quiet, with just a handful of quests enjoying the peace, waiting for the snows to come, usually later in the month. It's a great spot for guys—three squares a day, a small bar off the main house, Wi-Fi, and all the horseback riding you can handle. Tinhorn or saddle tramp, the ranch has you covered, with some horses one step away from the glue factory and others ready to race to the top of the ridge with a single spike of the spur.

We sit around and have a beer after the morning ride. We sip good whiskey before dinner—it helps soothe saddle sores and cranky backs. We light up a cigar on the porch of the rustic cabin we share, reminiscing late into the night, listening to the babbling brooks, cooing crickets and the wind. We talk about women, a lot. Some of us married our college sweethearts and are celebrating forty years of marriage. Divorce downed two of us and almost got another. One never married; one is on his third.

We never talk about money. We've all had some success in business. Some very, some hardly. And it wasn't necessarily the guys you would have predicted. A couple surprised us with how well they did. Some flew off to either coast. Some just worked hard, nose to the grindstone. Some never left the Midwest, all real butter and fresh corn on the cob.

Most all of us have experienced heartache. A lost love, a lost job or company, a life faded or tarnished somehow. Expectations unmet, missed. A married daughter in the grip of an affair brings tears and silence to the group when one of us whispers it out loud. The jokes stop and we all wonder how we escaped unscathed. But of course, we didn't. Something still hurts so bad we can't bear to share it in front of everyone. But maybe another time, after a few more beers. Maybe in a hushed conversation between only two of us.

Some of us have come to need and find the Lord over these past forty years. Some got close to him but faded away, waiting to latch on again. Some are still searching. That's okay; we've still got time. But time slips by quickly, falling like a rock from the top of the canyon, accelerating rapidly to hit the creek below. We don't preach to each other or judge one another. We just hang out, brothers forever.

We are men, among men, being men, reminiscing when we were boys. No girls allowed, no wives invited. If we need to howl at the moon, we howl. If we need to piss off the porch rail, we let it fly.

We gather to enjoy each other and the splendor of God's Wyoming. His red mountain majesty high, shedding His grace on all of us. Brothers forever.

Sometimes life feels so right, the sky so clear, the stars so bright and the company around you so friendly, you *know* Jesus is alive. You know the lumberjack is right next to you, enjoying the campfire, laughing at your stories, just one of the boys.

SCRIPTURE:

"Now the Lord had planted a garden in the east, in Eden; and there he put the man he had formed. And the Lord God made all kinds of trees grow out of the ground—trees that were pleasing to the eye and good for food. In the middle of the garden were the tree of life and the tree of the knowledge of good and evil. A river watering the garden flowed from Eden; from there is was separated into four headwaters."

—Genesis 2:8-10

PRAYER:

Thank you, Lord, for your majesty, your splendor, and the Earth you created. Let us handle it with care. Allow us to pause and take in what's beautiful all around us. Help us to see and marvel at your wonderful creation. And help us connect, heavenly Father, to those around us who need us, whether they cry out or not. Help us to feel their pain, share in their grief, celebrate their victories and anticipate their good health and well-being. Thank you, Lord, for the lifetime friendships and new friends to come. Open us to accept them all. Thank you, sweet Jesus. Amen.

Dreaming of a New Home

We wandered around the empty house for a few more moments. It was the last hour we would ever spend in the house that had been our home for fifteen years. Our kids weren't born while we lived in that house, but they'd grown up there. They went to high school and college, and then moved away on their own from that house. We'd spent the last month packing it up. Now the walls were bare, the furniture missing, the moving van long gone.

My wife and I meandered from room to room, capturing memories like fireflies in a glass jar. We wanted to store those good-time moments in our internal data banks so we wouldn't forget them. In the dining room, we remembered dinner parties with close friends and all those Thanksgivings with family.

In the kitchen, my wife reminisced about all the mother-daughter conversations, talking our daughter off the ledge in junior high, when girlfriends come and go as quickly as…well, junior high boyfriends.

In the large living room, we recalled that Saturday a decade or so ago when we renewed our weddings vows. Nicely decorated and rearranged, the room had resembled a tiny church ready for a ceremony. The pastor forgot the date and didn't show, but we improvised, spoke from our hearts and now we're more than halfway through our next twenty years.

In the backyard, we remembered pool parties, croquet matches, ladder tennis (look it up; it's a blast), sunsets, fireworks on the Fourth of July, the gopher invasion of '06, windstorms, and the time the diving board broke.

Upstairs, the little nook where we'd placed the roll-top desk that produced my first novel, frantically cranked out over a whirlwind three-month sprint. We cried in both kids' rooms. We could still see my athlete son's room, adorned with so many trophies, the shelves sagged under the weight, and the walls covered with photos of Michael Jordan, Steve Young and our son's three-sport high school teams. The tiny rubber basketball still hung from the pull cord of the ceiling fan like the last sentinel to days gone by.

We stopped at the door to my daughter's closet and spoke softly about what had hung there—dancer's outfits galore, glamorous prom dresses, big girl dress-up outfits for her cousins' visits, and the array of clothing styles she wore as she grew from little girl to young woman.

Downsizing dominated our family plans for a couple of years. The kids rarely visited, upkeep on the house had ratcheted up recently, and the three extra bedrooms collected only dust, not guests. Plus, we were ready. Ready for a new adventure, ready to relocate, ready to see what was next.

We'd traveled the West extensively, following our son's exploits playing college football. Among other places, we'd seen Boise, Vegas, Missoula, Portland, and San Diego and passed through more exotic remote towns like Coeur d'Alene, St. George and Sioux Falls. Every place displayed a unique culture, lifestyle and hominess. But no place felt like home.

The month before the house sold we concentrated our search on the California coast. Found a town that felt right, signed a lease on a condo, sold the home, attended going away tear-jerker parties, captured the memories, moved the dog and settled in. Wham, bam! Not quite spontaneous or impulsive, but certainly a little scary.

A little less than a year later as I write this, it still doesn't feel quite like home. We have cultivated a few friends, joined a gym, found the library, established a couple of favorite dinner spots and looked at dozens of homes to find our next one. But we still feel like nomads searching, wandering...

That unsettled feeling lingers just below the surface. We enjoy each day, but long for more permanence. In late night conversations, my wife and I talk dreamily about finding a new home. Not just a house, but also a place we can put down roots, dig into the soil, decorate the walls, rearrange the bookshelves, pick out the doormat.

When this adventure first began, I had to readjust my attitude. I like routine, established patterns, predictability. The adventure taught me more about expectation, excitement, and experience. I adapted—and at times, even reveled.

It's good to shake up life a bit when it becomes, for lack of a different word, a little lifeless. Most of us don't like too much change, but even a little change demands that we refocus our eyes. In routine, we miss the details after seeing them so often; in change, we see the fresh nuances. We notice the new sky, the new vegetation, the new smells and the new people with new attitudes.

But without a home, we begin to grumble in tiny ways. We're like cars with the front alignment a bit off. We wobble ever so slightly. Like ships at sea, the anchor bumping along the ocean floor, probing for a grip, a hold. Like a glider soaring with the wind at first, but as the current slows, we glance nervously at the terrain below in search of a landing spot. You get the idea.

I can imagine how the Israelites might have felt, searching for forty years for their promised land. They'd finally fled Egypt under miraculous circumstances, but didn't have a place to call home. Acting as God's instrument and spokesman, Moses maneuvered his people away from the pharaoh's clutch, through the Red Sea, heading east. Can you imagine how excited they all must have been? After hundreds of years in slavery, they were finally free. Sure, it must have been scary; some probably wanted to stay behind in the safety of routine life, even if the routine *was* slavery.

But God had bigger plans for His people. A new beginning, a new home, a new destiny. The adventure had begun—full of expectation and excitement.

But quickly the grumbling grew. The Israelites complained first of hunger, longing for the meat of their former lives. God delivered quail for the evenings and manna for the mornings. Then they complained of thirst, and God delivered water from the rocks of Horeb.

Quarrels, arguments and fights broke out among the desert travelers as fuses grew short and tempers flared. The longing for home, and just below the surface, uneasiness. God delivered again. This time, the Ten Commandments steered Moses and his selected tribesmen to dole out the laws and boundaries to live together and in peace. Laws to protect property, for justice and mercy, for social responsibility, even for festival celebration.

God was shaping and molding a people to test them and make them obey. To prepare them to carry on his vision. And yet the people still grumbled. Forty years is a long, long time. I get it. I'm rattled after less than one.

I don't think God has commandeered my life, set me adrift to test me and mold me. But He may be subtly directing my moves. I am in the desert, searching. I'm uneasy, a little unsettled. I long for the stability, safety and serenity of a real home. I want to plant my roots again into my own soil, watch them push down into the territory, spread out and grip tight. But the roots don't settle, don't dig down. They bump along the surface, sniffing for that spot that's just right.

Sometimes all you can do is trust God. Trust that He has a plan. One that's designed especially for you. Trust Him when you're roaming in the desert or floating at sea.

Jesus can be your anchor in times of wandering. He can always be home base. Olly, Olly, oxen free. Everybody can come to Jesus—for free. He may not immediately give you the answer you've been searching for, but He's never going to steer you in the wrong direction. He may be testing you or molding you. But that's not for me to say—that's between the two of you. If you're like me, the uncertainty can be unsettling. Or if you're the way I'd rather be, the searching and the wandering can be laced with excitement and wonder.

Take a few deep breaths. Smell the quail and the manna. Taste the clean crisp water. Keep your eyes focused on the horizon. Anticipate the promised land. And let Jesus lead you.

SCRIPTURE:

"See, I am sending an angel ahead of you to guard you along the way and to bring you to the place I have prepared. Pay attention to him and listen to what he says. Do not rebel against him; he will not forgive your rebellion, since my Name is in him."

—Exodus 23:20-21

PRAYER:

I surrender to you, Lord. Guide me, shape me, anyway you want me. Give me wonder and excitement. Take away the trepidation and trembling. Steady my hand, stabilize my feet. Help me to trust you, always. Fill my heart with your spirit and fill my thoughts with your son. Take away my grumbling and replace it with my praise. Thank you, sweet Jesus. Amen.

Testimony

John told his story as though he were reading a grocery list—matter of fact, nonchalant, no big deal.

Let's see. Bread, milk, butter.

"I was in the Navy, a helicopter pilot, in Vietnam."

Lettuce, lunchmeat, lentils.

"I was shot down, twice."

Coffee, beer, orange juice without the pulp.

"The second time we were hit, it didn't look good. I wasn't sure we were going to make it out alive."

Pasta, pasta sauce, fresh tomatoes, a little garlic.

"When things got hairy, I took a second and prayed. I told God if He got me out of this one alive, I'd dedicate my life to Him."

Apples, carrots, a few fresh peaches.

"And He did. And I did."

Coriander, dill, cinnamon…

"Wait, what?! You were shot down in Vietnam? Twice? And the second time, the only thing that saved you was *God*? How come I've never heard this story before, John?"

I'd known John for years. We went to the same church, met regularly for Bible studies, and shared many a meal together with our families. We'd met weekly for coffee, discussing our faith, our wives, our jobs—just life in general. We'd even been to a few sporting events together, quaffing a beer or two, letting our hair hang down, and enjoying each other's company.

But I'd never heard this story before, never heard his testimony.

My dad was in World War II, and I never once heard him talk about it. It wasn't until I was preparing his eulogy that my uncle told me of his service in the Pacific. How during the two years he was gone, my grandmother's hair had turned white from worry.

About the only story I've heard from my brother, who also served in Vietnam, was the day he landed in Southeast Asia. The company commander welcomed the new troops—most were drafted and many wanted to be anywhere else in the world except there. He delivered a list of do's and don'ts—keep your feet clean and your head down—and then asked the question that changed my brother's future. *Can anybody here type?*

My brother instinctively rejected the advice to never volunteer for anything and raised his hand. He served his year as the company clerk, close to combat but far enough away to be safe.

Many men who have fought in wars don't talk about it much. I never served, but I understand not wanting to relive an experience that daunting. Even if you weren't in harm's way, with bullets and bombs flying over your head, war stories are hard to express. Some stories remain unsaid, uncovered, buried.

But John was my close friend, and we were sharing our testimonies in a Bible study group. We were wrestling with why we couldn't express our faith easily. Sure, we knew that the way we treated people was almost as important as why we believed there was a God, but God talk is often difficult to discuss with others, especially nowadays when God seems to be out of favor in some circles. We suspected that if we could capture our testimony— our unique story of how God changed our lives—then those who didn't know God might ask questions when they heard it. We figured it was a great way to open up a conversation.

Remarkably, I discovered that most of us couldn't tell a compelling story. We rambled around, retelling how our families raised us, sent us to Sunday school, and instilled Christian values into our young lives. Some recanted the step-by-excruciating-step of how faith grew little by little over time. Or we detailed a life-altering experience as though we were reading from a grocery list. Like John. Most of our stories lacked zip, joy, and love—even when we knew the formula for a powerful testimony.

Don't know the formula? Here it is:
1. Your life before God.
2. The encounter with Jesus that changed your life.
3. How your life transformed after that encounter.

Let's apply the formula to his story. But remember, these are *my* words, not his. (Don't worry, he and I've discussed this; he gave me creative freedom to spice it up a bit, but it's all true. And, after all, his testimony did open up new conversations, didn't it?)

> ***John's life before God:*** I was raised in a Christian home, but I didn't practice Christianity much. I always knew what I should do, and sometimes I did it, but many times I did what I wanted to do. Nobody, not even Jesus, was going to tell me how to run my life. I

was full of piss and vinegar, my own man, a hard ass, a Navy pilot. I took care of myself and the men who served with me.

The encounter: We'd been shot down for the second time. We hoped like hell that air cover was coming to save us, but we weren't sure. There were injuries, bullets flying, and it looked like we might be captured—or killed. I had exhausted all my resources. There was nothing left for me to do. My last resort was Jesus. I told Him that if He got me out of this one, I'd dedicate the rest of my life to Him.

Life transformed: I now seldom put my wishes above Jesus. I serve him, not me. At church, at home, at the office, everywhere in my life. In response to that service, he gave me a loving wife when I didn't think it would ever happen. He delivered to us two wonderful children when that looked virtually impossible. He cured me from two bouts with cancer. I'm still a hard ass, but a hard ass with a soft heart for others.

Now, let me guess what you're thinking. "That's a nice rephrasing of his story—and it is certainly more powerful and may lead to questions about Jesus—but *I* wasn't shot down in Vietnam. I don't have a life-altering event that I can talk about." That's what you were thinking, right?

Think harder.

Or maybe you're thinking: "Well, I've known Jesus my whole life. I accepted him when I was young. I've never known a life without Jesus, so I really can't think about your formula because I can't make those distinctions like the 'encounter' or the 'transformation.'"

I repeat, think harder.

If you really believe in the power of Christ, if you have a faith that He is the hope of the world, and you can't say how He's changed your life, then maybe He hasn't. If you've known Jesus all your life and cannot pinpoint when you met Him and how He altered the course of your life, maybe you need to meet Him all over again. If we can't emphatically tell our testimony story so that people want to hear more, maybe it's time to get back in touch with Him and ask for His Help.

There's an analogy in sales. Ever heard of the elevator speech? Sales trainers teach that you have to be able to engage a customer with the benefits of your product quickly, in the average time of a typical elevator ride, about thirty seconds. Your sales elevator speech has to be succinct, powerful, and meaningful.

Here's my elevator *testimony* speech.

I was raised in a church, attending every week, but I never knew much about Jesus. During and after college, I got as far away from the church and

Jesus as possible—in every aspect of my life—including drinking, drugs, and sex. I'd been sexually abused as a young boy, and the guilt and shame I felt was exploding out of me in anger, resentment, and tons of self-doubt and self-loathing. Even after joining a church and accepting Jesus as my savior, I couldn't find a release for that shame.

Finally, Christ came to me and told me that the person I was now wasn't the way He'd made me. And if I gave Him that guilt, that shame, and that self-loathing, He'd nail them all to the cross. That I'd be a new person, the one He'd originally made. So I did—I let go—and I finally began to heal.

Read it again. Time it if you want. It takes about thirty seconds. Apply the formula to it. It works, doesn't it? It didn't take me long to write that paragraph, because I've practiced it many times. I've delivered it in front of Bible study groups, friends, relatives and a few larger audiences. (I still tear up almost every time I tell it.)

I have a thirty second version, a three-minute version, and if people are interested—some are, some aren't—a ten-minute version with all the details. Some people don't want to hear the longer story; after all, even if I leave out the gory details, which I do, it's still a pretty heavy story. But it's never boring.

Again, you're thinking, "I wasn't abused; I didn't need that kind of healing." Or you're thinking, "I'm not a storyteller. I don't even like to talk about myself."

And again I say, better get in touch with the man upstairs.

Evangelism isn't for all of us. It's not everyone's gift. But we all have a story to tell and a world of people dying, literally, to hear it. If your story is a little dull, or it's lost its power, or you've told it so many times it sounds more like a grocery list than an encounter with the Most High God, maybe it's time to go back to the drawing board. Give it a little flavor, spice it up, make it sizzle a bit. And as you work with the formula, you may discover your God all over again. You may re-discover why you fell in love with Him in the first place. Why He found you, why He saved you, and how that encounter changed your life. Won't that be sweet?

You never know when you'll be in that elevator, when that opportunity presents itself. When that somebody God has placed beside you desperately—life or death—needs to hear your story. Don't miss the opportunity; don't be unprepared. And don't read your grocery list.

Make it sing!

SCRIPTURE:

"Hear this, all you peoples;
  listen, all who live in the world,
both low and high,
  rich and poor alike:
My mouth will speak words of wisdom;
  the utterance from my heart will give understanding.
I will turn my ear to a proverb; with the harp I will expound my riddle."

—Psalm 49:1-4

PRAYER:

May the words of my mouth and the meditation of my heart be pleasing to you, Lord. When I stumble or fall or ramble, speak to me. Speak through me, Lord. When I lack the words or miss the feeling, touch me and tell me again how much you love me. Search my heart and make your ways known to me, Father. I want to tell your story. I want to tell *my* story. I want to be your servant. Most times, I need your help. I'm unable to do this on my own. I need you, Lord. I love you, Lord. Help me. Please. Thank you, sweet Jesus. Amen.

The Adam in Me

I want the girl. Not *my* girl. The other one.

I want the second drink. And the third. Maybe the fourth.

I want the bad apple, not the good one. I want a taste, just a taste, mind you, of the wicked one. Not all the time, not every day, but I want it. It's part of me; it's inside me. It's something I can't control. It's not really me at all, at least I don't think it is. It feels like an evil twin living inside me that only comes out occasionally.

Most of the time I can control it. Most, but not all. I usually have the strength to avoid giving in, to beat it down, to keep it in check. But that evil twin is always there, lurking, just below the surface. Let's call him Adam. Named after the Adam we meet in the garden.

As I've grown older, I've gotten to know myself better. I know my strengths and weaknesses. I've taken Myers-Briggs and a dozen other personality tests. I've got them all stored in a notebook somewhere. For a while, I studied them once or twice a year. They're all now committed to memory, for the most part.

Recently, I even found a new one I'd never seen before; it gauged my "emotional intelligence." I could have told you I wouldn't score real high on that one. You can always teach this old dog a new trick or two, but mostly I revert back to all the tricks I've ever known.

I have quite a few strengths, actually. I'd list them all here, but I have a feeling you're really not interested. You have just as many as I do, maybe more. You've learned to recognize yours—and play to them. You can see the strengths of other people, too. Maybe you have a boss or a spouse or a friend who is full of strengths. Maybe they have one special asset that you lack—being a good listener, great with numbers, patience, humility. You envy them that one special strength, even emulate these individuals if you can. You practice and practice and eventually, you get better at that trait. It may never become your strength, but now you can use it to your advantage.

It's really my weaknesses you're interested in. You have just as many as I do, maybe more. You want to see how I've overcome mine. What I did to banish them, beat them into submission, or how I turned that weakness into a strength.

For instance, I'm not too good with numbers, so I took an accounting class. It was called something like "basic accounting for non-accounting managers." Accounting for dummies. I got better, but it's not my strength and never will be.

Then I wanted to learn something brand new; something I had no affinity or talent for. So I taught myself to juggle. I always had decent hand-eye coordination, but nothing like it takes to juggle. I bought three hacky sacks, the small footbags that young kids use to practice their soccer skills. I sequestered myself in a small room and just tossed them up in the air.

For a month, they flew all over that room and bounced off the walls, but eventually I figured it out. Now I can juggle—big deal, huh?—but it's never going to be something I'll get paid for at the state fair or the ocean pier.

I have other weaknesses. I can't sing, for instance. Couldn't carry a tune in a bucket. Can't draw, either; never graduated from stick figures. I'd love to play an instrument. I tried piano and trumpet in grade school and failed miserably at both. I bought a guitar in my twenties. It's still around here somewhere, gathering dust, but it's not producing any noticeable music.

But those really aren't the weaknesses you're interested in. You want to know how I conquer lust, or greed, or jealousy. The biggies. Maybe you have one or two all your own, the weaknesses you just can't seem to get a good firm handle on. They used to be called vices; maybe that's too old school. Sins? Nah, too nebulous, too hard to define—can't most everything be a sin if it's overdone or underdone?

Let's stick with the word *weaknesses*. Remember in the old Superman movies when Superman would get a whiff of Kryptonite? He'd go weak in the knees, lose his strength, and literally fall down on his face. We all have our Kryptonite, don't we? Maybe not quite as bad as the Man of Steel, but bad just the same. What's yours? Alcohol, drugs, porn? It's something we can't control.

I had a friend whose wife was an alcoholic. He always said she craved "the buzz," that she had no control over the craving. I feel her pain. Once, when I was drinking too much, I swore off all alcohol for ninety-nine days. The first week or so, I really missed it—that's when I knew I had a problem. But I went back to the booze—that's what my dad called it; he had the problem, too. I crave the buzz. I can control it, but I still crave it. Damn!

Lust is another one I struggle with. If Jimmy Carter was right, that we commit adultery in our hearts if we lust, then I'm guilty. In thirty-one years of marriage, I've never committed actual adultery. Never even came close; never kissed another woman, never touched another woman. But I can't seem to control that lust factor, the one where I force myself to turn away from the pretty woman, the half-naked breast, the scantily clad model. I tend to turn *towards*, not away. I can control it, but not completely. I never act on that urge, but it acts on me.

I've tried drugs, too. I was a child of the 1960s. What can I say? I inhaled. I did a few hallucinogens in college, snorted a little coke in the 80s. I had a buddy who liked to imbibe even more than I did. He tried heroin once and said it was the most exquisite feeling in the world. He understood how easy it would be to get hooked on it. I stayed away.

Luckily, these weaknesses don't crush me. And I suppose you'd let me off the hook if you knew how much I'd battled them. *After all*, you'd say, *don't be so hard on yourself; we all have them, that's what makes us human.*

I'd say, *thanks for understanding, that means a lot to me.* That would be true; it would make it better—for a while. But it really wouldn't help me much, would it?

They used to call that co-dependence. Don't get me wrong; I'm not blaming you. They are *my* weaknesses after all.

Here's a better way to talk to me about my weaknesses. Don't tell me to cut back. Tell me to cut it out. Don't tell me to be strong. Tell me to be a man. Don't tell me to expect to get better. Tell me to excise it all together. Don't sympathize or empathize. Exorcise!

I'm not a role model. I understand when a professional athlete blurts out, *Don't have your kids look up to me. My job isn't being a role model.*

What they're really saying is: *I'm not good enough for that. I'm not strong enough.* I get it; me, neither.

I'll fight back, that's for sure. I'll put on my full armor of God. My belt, my helmet and shield. I'll wield my sword, stick out my breastplate, and fight the good fight. But I'm going to lose, at least some of the time. Nobody wins all the time against their demons, do they?

I'm not a goody-two-shoes. I'm not even a goody-one-shoe. It's more like I'm barefoot, with calluses, a little athlete's foot and toenail fungus. I'm nowhere close to being like the apostle Paul, if you're even thinking in that direction. He was an apostle; I'm a reprobate in comparison. He had a thorn in his side, always afflicted, never whole. I'm in the middle of an entire thorn bush—sometimes with absolutely no means of escape.

Sure, I pray. All the time, at times. Sure, I cry out; often, it seems. Yes, He answers—every single time in some way or another. Every once in a while though, I feel I'm barely hanging on. Hanging off a precipice, clinging to my strengths—Him, His promises, His word—and being nipped at from below. Raising my legs, trying my best not to get bitten or devoured by the demon below, as my hand clings to the ledge. Fingers cramping, fingernails digging in, arms tiring, almost wanting to give up, let go, succumb.

But I cling. The Adam in me urges me not to fight so hard. Indulge once in a while.

He says to me:

You want that girl. Not your girl. The other one.

You want that second drink. And the third. Maybe the fourth.

What's it going to hurt? Just this once. Take a bite of that apple. No, not that one—the bad one.

But still I cling, often only by a thread. After all, I'm only human. But Jesus is God, my savior, my lumberjack. So I cry out to Him, "Help me, sweet Jesus!" And He always hears me, He always answers. He's always just a whisper away. Listening. Ready. And then I whisper back, "Thank you, sweet Jesus. Amen."

Cry out to Him. He's listening for you, too.

SCRIPTURE:

"He reached down from on high and took hold of me;
> he drew me out of deep waters.
He rescued me from my powerful enemy,
> from my foes, who were too strong for me.
They confronted me in the day of my disaster,
> but the Lord was my support.
He brought me out into a spacious place;
> he rescued me because he delighted in me.
The Lord has dealt with me according to my righteousness;
> according to the cleanness of my hands he has rewarded me."

—Psalm 18:16-20

PRAYER:

I need you, Lord, more than I'll ever admit. I want to go it alone, prove my worth, and be a man. But I'm weak, ineffective. The world keeps beckoning and I keep listening. Sometimes I fall; sometimes I stand tall. But mostly I fall. Help me, heavenly Father. Please. I can't make it without you. I know that deep down inside me that I need you. It's hard to show my vulnerability, sometimes even with you. Rescue me, wrap your arms around me, comfort me, love me. I will never be able to thank you enough in this lifetime, Lord. Keep me on my knees. Keep me softhearted. Help me to be broken-hearted over the things that break your heart. And help me, Lord, to stand tall again. Thank you, sweet Jesus. Amen.

Afterward

I love alter calls. My wife Nancy and I came to know Christ in an evangelical church and most every service ended with an alter call. An opportunity to give your life to Christ.

In most every alter call I've witnessed, the process is simple. The preacher usually says something like this: "If you confess your sins, ask for forgiveness and accept Christ as your Lord and Savior, you will be reborn. A new person, a child of God. Just pray this simple prayer…"

The process to become a child of God is easy. The journey to live a life changed by God is not.

Some people believe that they are Christians because they prayed that simple alter call prayer. Others believe they are Christians because they go to church regularly, or they give to organizations that help people around the world, or because they are good people, or that they have forgone a sinful pleasure. Many think that because they read the Bible, they are Christians.

But the Bible says that we must change. Change to become like Christ—that makes us Christians, followers of Christ. When we accept Christ as our Lord, he somehow, supernaturally, enters our heart and begins to change it. He gives us his Spirit to guide us to an eternal life with God.

But to think we magically become victorious over sins simply because of that process is a grave mistake.

You've read in these pages how I've written about my struggles to live a life devoted to Christ. It's not easy, and it's not simple. Far from it. There have been many times when I've wanted the easy path to eternal life, but I haven't been willing to give up my ways. I thought that the simple vow of confession and then dedication would change me. But that's the devil's lie. Only Christ in my heart can change me. Or change you. And to become Christians, we must change.

If you want eternal life with Christ in heaven, there is a way. I want you to consider—and decide—if that way is for you.

I'll borrow the process outlined by Billy Graham, perhaps the world's most influential evangelist, from his book *The Reason for My Hope*.

1) You must be convinced that you need Christ. If you think you can live your life just fine without Him, thank you very much, with you in the pilot's seat flying strictly under your own power, then you will never find Christ. Jesus did not demand that you come to Him. He invited you. But you will need to confess your spiritual need to let Christ lead.

2) You need to understand the message of the cross. Christ died for you and me. He was the sacrifice for our sins. He was betrayed, beaten, and nailed to a cross because He loved you and gave himself up for you. The cross was the way back for all of us to God—the only way.

3) You need to weigh the cost of this decision. In the Gospels, the story of the young man who is often referred to as the rich, young ruler illustrates this point. When he comes expectantly to Jesus asking what he has to do for eternal life, Jesus says: "sell everything you have, give it all to the poor, take up the cross and follow me." That is not the path to salvation, but it *is* one to eternity. Give it all up, let Christ lead. You need to give up your ways. All of your ways, the world's ways. Follow Christ. For many people, that's too much to give up. Is it too much for you?

4) You must confess that Jesus is the Lord of your life. If you do that in front of others, then your commitment is even more definite. If you only make that declaration in the silence of your heart, it will be too easy to break your promise.

5) You must be *willing* for Christ to change your life. It won't happen all at once. It didn't for me. Ten years after asking God to run my life, I finally met Lumberjack Jesus at my dining room table and understood what I needed to relinquish—my guilt and shame—so I could be free to live the way Christ wanted. Once you become willing, Satan will make it harder for you to keep that commitment. Just a warning. Ask for help, you'll need it.

6) You must want nourishment from God's Word. By reading, listening, praying, talking and absorbing the Bible, then you will grow towards a life like Christ's. Get the good book and find a church to help you understand it. Go ahead, jump in.

Would you like eternal life?

Would you like to know that all your sins are forgiven?

Would you like to meet and know God, Lumberjack Jesus, face to face?

It's simple. It's easy. Just pray the simple prayer below.

SCRIPTURE:

"Then Jesus declared, 'I am the bread of life. He who comes to me will never go hungry, and he who believes in me will never be thirsty. For my

Father's will is that everyone who look to the Son and believes in him shall have eternal life...' "

—John 6:35 & 40

Prayer:

O heavenly father, I am a sinner. I repent of those sins and ask for your forgiveness. Help me to turn away from what keeps me from you. I acknowledge your sacrifice on the cross. Come into my life. Be my Lord and Savior. Give me the faith and trust to believe you always—and follow you always. Thank you for your Son. Thank you for saving me. Thank you for loving me. In Jesus' sweet name. Amen.

Now get ready for the journey. God bless you.

Dear Reader,

I hope you enjoyed *Lumberjack Jesus* and that some of my roadblocks will make your journey easier. If you'd like to leave a review, please feel free to share your comments of the book where you purchased your copy. To learn more about me or read my blog, please visit my website at BKirkpatrick. com. I'll leave you with this short excerpt of my next novel, *Booneville, A Love Story...*

God bless you.
Bruce Kirkpatrick

Chapter One

Johnny Roe caught himself staring at Suzanne McLean; she was shapely and young enough to look really good in that black miniskirt. Johnny knew she was only twenty-nine years old, but she sure had a knack for holding an audience. She was about halfway through her pitch, a presentation to him and the executive team illustrating how she would position their newest client at the ad agency in what everybody knew was a competitive, crowded marketplace.

Johnny's thoughts wandered from Suzanne's miniskirt to a conversation he'd had with his wife that morning. It wasn't like she was mad at him, or even annoyed. It felt more like disinterest. *How in the world could his wife be disinterested in his business and their life together?* Was that what was really happening, or was he imagining it all? He had tried to talk about the kids and what was on their schedules over the next several days but all he got was a nod or a shrug. She even turned her head when he said an early goodbye that morning, and all he got was the proverbial peck on the cheek instead of a kiss on the lips.

Johnny tried to not look bored, even with the flare that Suzanne exuded with the presentation. He'd been at the agency ten years and he'd seen a lot of presentations. Most of the time, when account managers like McLean presented ideas, 95 percent of them were shit. Textbook kind of ideas that had been done 100 times before, with limited success and even less imagination. The true creative ideas came from the whole process. First you did the research, then you did the competitive comparison, then you got down as many ideas as you could. After the exhaustive download of creativity, he usually had to let it simmer for a while. It was rare that the one, bright shining moment of brilliance popped out and lay there on the table to be discovered. More times than not, it lay hidden beneath a layer or two or seven, and you had to peel away the accumulation, bit-by-bit, piece-by-piece.

Everyone outside of advertising thought that creativity was simple, especially those that had a creative idea every once or twice. Just get it down, spice it up, and blast the hell out of it—easy-peasy. But guys who ran ad agencies knew that the process—the long, long process to find that nugget rarely came easy. Like that old Ringo song, "It Don't Come Easy".

So as an excited Suzanne McLean peaked for her crescendo, Johnny doodled. Words or phrases mostly. He would take an idea from a phrase he'd heard, maybe it came from Suzanne—at least he'd give her credit for it if the idea panned out—and just doodle with it. Reverse it, add to it, subtract from it, change one word, then the other. Use the built-in thesaurus in his brain. It was all part of the process. Roe always used a pencil, never a pen. Always a note pad, never a computer. Who the hell could doodle on a computer anyway? He liked the feel of the graphite lead as it slid along the paper. About once a quarter, he bought a small box of Ticonderoga pencils. Yellow pencils with pink erasers. He loved their slogan—The World's Best Pencil—and thought that any company that had the balls to call themselves the best in the whole world deserved his business.

His agency, Troubadour (not Troubadour Communications or Troubadour Agency, just Troubadour), had won the business of a new company in the social media world that was going to make a killing on the web. Or so they said. Troubadour's job was to at least make them relative, so that some over-agitated biggy in the business saw enough of a threat that they'd gobble them up, making instant zillionaires of the founders and putting most of the rest of the underlings back into the ranks of the unemployed.

Plan B was to go public with a stock offering. The IPO market was gradually coming back from the brink during the great recession and within a year or eighteen months should be overripe with money to heap boatloads onto a snazzy, little social media gem.

As he was lost in doodle world, Johnny's iPhone buzzed. He had it on mute, but the text message from his administrative assistant, Laura, made the little machine shimmy across the table.

The text read: Need to talk to you NOW!!!

With shouty caps and three exclamation points no less. This could be important. *We'll see.* If she stuck her head into the conference room in less than two minutes, he'd excuse himself and see what she wanted. If she waited until the meeting broke up, Johnny would tell her to tone down the exclamation points.

As soon as he began to put pencil again to paper, Laura opened the conference room door and searched for eye contact with him. She looked ashen, her eyes darted past him once, did a wild search of the room, then settled back and focused on him again. She motioned abruptly with her hand to come outside and the pleading look in her eyes conveyed a sense of real urgency. Johnny immediately said a soft "excuse me" to Suzanne and hustled to the door.

Laura couldn't keep eye contact with him. "There's someone here to see you," she said.

"For this, you had to call me out," Johnny teased, trying to add a bit of levity to the moment.

Laura just stared at her desk and fidgeted with her hair. One reason Johnny had hired the middle-aged Laura Ainsley was her ability to keep cool under almost any circumstance. Cool as the other side of the pillow, he often quoted to her, and always as a compliment. He'd never seen her rattled, but at the moment, he could see her hands shake as she straightened out the papers on her desk.

"A Mr. Worth is in the lobby."

There's something she isn't telling me.

"Okay, show him to my office."

Laura nodded. Still no eye contact.

"All righty then," Johnny said almost under his breath as he slipped across the hall to his office.

He walked around his big desk and took a quick look out his 11th floor window at another gorgeous San Francisco morning, glancing at the blue of the bay and the swash of color from the adjoining buildings as he took a deep breath. American flags flew atop several buildings, flapping wildly with the onshore breeze. Tiny white caps in the bay signaled wind direction and small sailing boats bobbed slowly about, almost in slow motion.

"Mr. Roe?"

"Yes sir."

"My name is Osmund Worth."

Johnny wanted to say *nice to meet you*, but his mouth wasn't working. The clothes the man was wearing…

"Mr. Roe, perhaps you should sit down. I have some terrible news. I'm the deputy county coroner."

Acknowledgements

When I published my first book, I didn't thank enough people. I mistakenly thought most of that accomplishment came from my own hand. I was pretty proud of it. I won't make that mistake this time.

So many people have contributed to the person I am today—and this book is a reflection of that person—that if I listed them all it would resemble the genealogy that opens the New Testament in Matthew. I usually skip over that part, so here I won't list all the people; I'll cut to the chase.

I'm deeply grateful to all the folks at Fremont Community Church in Fremont, California. I entered their doors back in the early '90s and their patience, sincerity, and love gave me a rebirth. Literally. Thanks Pastor Sherman. To the rest of that congregation: I'll never forget you.

Over the years, I've been a part of several small group Bible studies. All have been deeply important to me, but the men and women of Community Presbyterian Church in Danville, CA, are in the DNA of who I am today. I've never laughed so much or cried so hard as I did with them. They molded this heap of clay; they heard most all of these stories. I miss them every day and lament that I will probably never experience that kind of love again on this planet. Thank you Katrina and Rich Lambert, Judy and Dave Rohrbach, Patty Walker, Lori Larsen, Deborah and Terry Campbell, Nancy Nelson, Kathy and Patrick Jones, Melanie and Frank Carbrey, Jane and Jim Vawter, and Cara and Mike Iverson.

A special shoutout to Rita vanRijn Stensgaard who helped teach me to express my love for Jesus—and for others, too. This book would have languished in unexpressed anguish if not for you.

Thanks to Dave Rohrbach for the first read. You pointed me in the right direction and helped me hear what I wasn't hearing before.

I so appreciate the contribution to this book that my original editors, Virginia McCullough and Lynda McDaniel of The Book Catalysts, have made. They took rambling writings and ill-conceived ideas and helped me craft them into stories. I stuttered and misspoke—and they clarified my voice. Let's work together again soon.

To Brittiany Koren, you made it all so much better, down to the last detail.

The clan of Kirkpatricks that I belong to have been in America for a long time, but time has scattered us all across the country. To those of you who know these stories, I thank you for your understanding and patience as I battled my demons. For those who are reading them for the first time, I'm sorry I haven't known you better and I trust you'll extend the same love.

To my children, Conor and Kelley, you lived most every story in the book with me. Thanks for loving me when I wasn't my best. Thanks for loving me when I was my very worst. Thanks for forgiving past mistakes; I'm probably not done making them, so I'll need you to extend the father warranty a while longer.

If ever there was a model of grace incarnate, it's my wife, Nancy. You've read about her in several stories in this book, but she's more than part of me. She *is* me, we are one. Thank you, hon, for showing me the way, forgiving me when I detoured or lost the path entirely, and for loving me no matter what. You are the closest thing to Jesus with skin on that I could ever hope to encounter this side of heaven. I love you, Nan.

And especially, first and foremost, *número uno*, above and beyond, thank you, Lumberjack Jesus.

And all God's children said: Amen!

About the Author

Bruce Kirkpatrick spent over thirty years in Silicon Valley as an executive and entrepreneur. Since his move to Southern California, he now divides his time between writing and serving on nonprofit boards of directors, including Christian Education Development Company and Extollo International. His nonprofit work includes helping to train Haitian men and women in employable skills, so that they can find jobs, feed their families and have hope for the future. His first novel, *Hard Left*, was published in 2007.

Please visit Bruce's website at BKirkpatrick.com to learn more about the author and his books.

CPSIA information can be obtained
at www.ICGtesting.com
Printed in the USA
FSHW02n1718210818
51443FS